NEWBURY   BACK YARD

CAMBRIDGE—Newbury

THE ROYAL HORTICULTURAL SOCIETY

GARDENER'S
FIVE YEAR
RECORD
BOOK

1993 —

THE ROYAL HORTICULTURAL SOCIETY

GARDENER'S FIVE YEAR RECORD BOOK

COMPILED BY
DONALD McKENDRICK

EBURY PRESS STATIONERY

PICTURE CREDITS

JANUARY
A Winter Garden – Joseph Farquarson (Fine Art Picture Library)
FEBRUARY
In the Garden – Bertha Wegmann (© Christie's)
MARCH
A Cottage Garden – James Matthews (courtesy of Church Street Gallery) (Fine Art Picture Library)
APRIL
A Cottage Garden – G. H. Hughes (courtesy of Anthony Mitchell, Nottingham) (Fine Art Picture Library)
MAY
Abbey Leix, Eire – Ernest Arthur Rowe (Christopher Wood Gallery) (The Bridgeman Art Library)
JUNE
A Summer Herbaceous Border – Lilian Stannard (Christopher Wood Gallery) (The Bridgeman Art Library)
JULY
The Lily Border at Tagley Manor – Thomas H. Hunn (Christopher Wood Gallery) (The Bridgeman Art Library)
AUGUST
View of a Country House and Garden – Ernest Arthur Rowe (Christopher Wood Gallery) (The Bridgeman Art Library)
SEPTEMBER
Late September – Lilian Stannard (courtesy of Bonhams) (The Bridgeman Art Library)
OCTOBER
Abberton Church from Rous Lench Court – Ernest Arthur Rowe (Christopher Wood Gallery)
(The Bridgeman Art Library)
NOVEMBER
An Amateur (watercolour) – Frederick Walker (British Museum, London) (The Bridgeman Art Library)
DECEMBER
Autumn Morning – John Atkinson Grimshaw (Christopher Wood Gallery) (The Bridgeman Art Library)

Cover: Border 1790's, probably Mulhouse factory France. Reproduced courtesy of Board of Trustees, Victoria and Albert Museum

First published in 1992 by Ebury Press Stationery
An imprint of the Random Century Group
Random Century House, 20 Vauxhall Bridge Road,
London SW1V 2SA

Set in Goudy Old Style Roman
by 🅐 Tek Art Ltd., Addiscombe, Croydon, Surrey
Printed in Italy

Designed by Peter Butler

ISBN 0 09175 136 5

INTRODUCTION

This *Gardener's Five Year Record Book*, a new publication from the Royal Horticultural Society, offers you an opportunity to create your own unique record of your garden and gardening achievements.

Part of the fascination of gardening is that no two years are the same. Each season brings its own variations on the year before – it may be drier, wetter, hotter or cooler – and this in turn will affect what plants flower well and when, as well as fruit and vegetable harvesting times and when basic cultivations and seed sowings are carried out. At the end of five years, your personal record book will be an invaluable guide to future planning as well as a useful memory jogger.

To promote the enjoyment of gardening to an ever-increasing audience has been a major aim of the Society since its foundation in 1804. In the early years the Society, and its plant hunters such as David Douglas and Robert Fortune, led the way in the search for new species in many countries of the world; our rich and varied gardens of today are a tribute to these and other enterprising men who faced danger and hardships to bring back such fine garden plants as *Garrya elliptica*, *Ribes sanguineum*, *Jasminum multiflorum* and *Platycodon grandiflorus*.

The Royal Horticultural Society has become the world's leading authority on all that is best in horticulture as well as the most popular society for professional and amateur gardeners, with more than 150,000 members. It is active in promoting lectures, demonstrations and flower shows, including London's Chelsea Flower Show. The Society's Garden at Wisley in Surrey is renowned for its seasonal displays and its work in the science and craft of gardening. An equally inspiring garden at Rosemoor in Devon is a more recent creation and part of the programme of progressive development that will take the Royal Horticultural Society into the 21st century and the celebration of its bicentenary.

For information on the Royal Horticultural Society contact:
The Secretary,
The Royal Horticultural Society,
80, Vincent Square,
LONDON SW1P 2PE

The gardens at Wisley are open every day of the year
except Christmas Day (10 a.m. – sunset). Sundays are for Royal
Horticultural Society members only.

Rosemoor is open every day except Christmas Day (10 a.m. – sunset)

The Lindley Library, 80 Vincent Square is open
Monday to Friday 9.30 a.m. – 5.00 p.m.

JANUARY

In the Bleak mid-winter
Frosty wind made moan,
Earth stood hard as iron,
Water like a stone.

CHRISTINA ROSSETTI
MID-WINTER

A Winter Garden
Joseph Farquarson

JANUARY

WEEK 1

WEATHER _____

OUTSIDE

   VEGETABLES _____

   FRUIT _____

   FLOWERS _____

   BULBS _____

   SHRUBS/TREES _____

   LAWNS _____

GREENHOUSE _____

NOTES _____

YEAR (Cambridge) 1993

New Year's Day Cold Snap - from 50° down to 15° on Sat. 1/2 AM.

1/4 -5 High 50's - 60, Heavy Showers on 1/5. Witch Hazel blooming in Cemetary

5 - 6 Cool

__1998__
   NEWBURY
1. 30.55↑, 0° brisk W, clear High of 18° late PM
2. 30.25↑, 28°, cldy
3. 30.30↓, 35° mild, cldy High in 50's, sunny
4. 30.40↑, 44°, ptly cldy, calm
5 - 6 away
7. 30.40, 32°, drizzly, occ. heavier rain, mid 30's all day

YEAR (Newbury) 1994

Cold.

Heavy snow on Jan. 4 and 6

Juncos, Chickadees, Mourning Doves, RB + WB Nuthatch, Tree Sparrows, Cardinals, Mocking Bird, Hairy + Downy Woodpeckers, Starlings, Purple Finches

YEAR 1995	YEAR 1996	YEAR 1997
New Year's Day: Heavy rain, upper 30s	New Year's Day: 30-13↓ cloudy, a few flurries. Same birds. No titmice, No Jay.	New Year's Day: -4°F at dawn, clear, calm
2 Heavy rain → heavy snow	2. Cold. 2" light snow. NE storm begins at night	2 Milder
7 More heavy rain	3 15° at dawn. About 7" on the ground. Snow continues. Another 3" by noon. Wonderful ♀ Cooper's Hawk in Walski's maple!	3 - 4 Drizzly, foggy, sleet, ice 30s to 40s
	4 10° at dawn. Ocean effect snow. - another 1½". Clear, cold.	5 40s, fog
	5 0° at dawn. Clear. Cold front in PM, gusty.	6 Turns colder, blue sky
	6 -5° at dawn. Clear. +10 the high for the day. gusty NW wind	7 33° the high blustery NW
	7 0° at dawn. Cloudy. Juncos, Chickadees, Mourning Doves, RB+WBN at hotel, Tree Sparrows, Cardinals, Mocking Bird, Downy W., Starlings, P. Finches, goldfinches	8 To London & Africa! Clear, cool.

JANUARY

WEEK 2

WEATHER _____

OUTSIDE

VEGETABLES _____

FRUIT _____

FLOWERS _____

BULBS _____

SHRUBS/TREES _____

LAWNS _____

GREENHOUSE _____

NOTES _____

YEAR Cambridge 1993

7 All snow from December gone

9 Cold - High of 25°. Raw NE wind.

10 12° at dawn. Moved compost.

13 3" Snow
14 Another 3-4"

Juncos, white throats, Cardinals, Finches, Mockingbird, Starlings, Crows

YEAR Newbury 1994

8 Heavy snow

11 -5°F at 6AM

13 Warm spell - 35°

14 Flurries

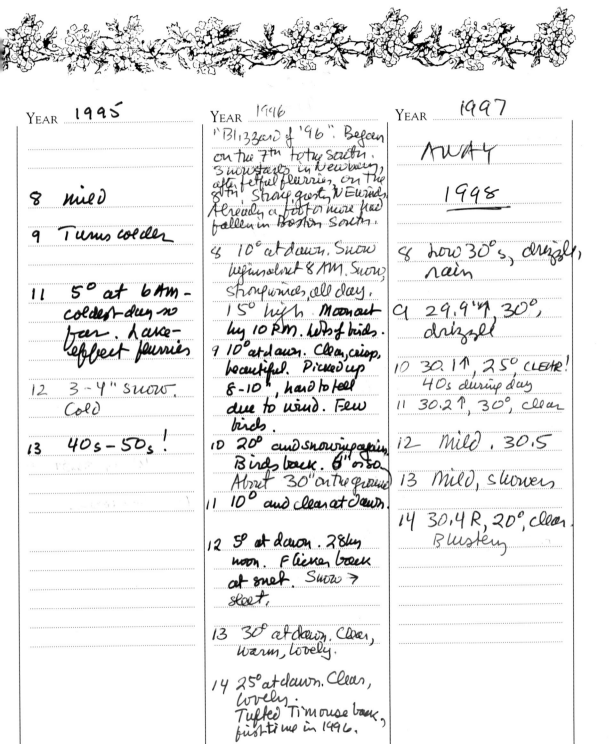

YEAR 1995

8 mild

9 Turns colder

11 5° at 6 AM -
    coldest day so
    far. Lake-
    effect flurries

12 3-4" snow.
    Cold

13 40s - 50s !

YEAR 1996

"Blizzard of '96". Began
on the 7th to the south.
3 inches in Newbury,
after fitful flurries, on the
8th. Strong, gusty N.E. winds.
Already a foot or more had
fallen in Boston south.

8 10° at dawn. Snow
   begins about 8 AM. Snow,
   strong winds, all day.
   15° high. Moon out
   by 10 PM. Lots of birds.

9 10° at dawn. Clear, crisp,
   beautiful. Picked up
   8-10", hard to tell
   due to wind. Few
   birds.

10 20° and snowing again.
    Birds back. 6" or so.
    About 30" on the ground.

11 10° and clear at dawn.

12 5° at dawn. 28 by
    noon. Flicker back
    at suet. Snow →
    sleet.

13 30° at dawn. Clear,
    warm, lovely.

14 25° at dawn. Clear,
    lovely.
    Tufted Timouse back,
    first time in 1996.

YEAR 1997

AWAY

1998

8 Low 30's, drizzle,
   rain

9 29.9"↑, 30°,
   drizzle

10 30.1↑, 25° CLEAR!
    40s during day

11 30.2↑, 30°, clear

12 Mild. 30.5

13 Mild, showers

14 30.4 R, 20°, clear.
    Blustery

Ground snow-covered
since 12/14/95. Above
freezing last time - 12/31 !

JANUARY

WEEK 3

WEATHER _____

OUTSIDE
  VEGETABLES _____

  FRUIT _____

  FLOWERS _____

  BULBS _____

  SHRUBS/TREES _____

  LAWNS _____

GREENHOUSE _____

NOTES _____

YEAR — Cambridge 1993

15 Warmed up,
all snow melted
by end of week

YEAR — Newbury 1994

15 Another cold
Snap.

Redpolls at feeder

16 −10°F at
dawn. Warmed
to −3° by noon,
to +4 by 2:00
Tufted Titmouse

17 Light snow in AM
Rain overnight,
40° by dawn

18 Turns colder.
−3° by dawn on
19th.

2 Rabbit along
tree line between
us + Walshes

YEAR 1995	YEAR 1996	YEAR 1997
		AWAY
		<u>1998</u>
15 O ver 60	15 30 at dawn, falling during clear day	15 30.65, 12°, calm morning + becoming cldy
16 Same – Tropical shower, some sun	16 5° at dawn.	16 30.1"F 30°F, snow, b'casts. About 6" in all, wet, ice on pavements.
	17 Icy top burns off, 50° for a high	
		17 29.95R, 20°, clear, lovely.
Away for balance of month.	18 Warm – 50's	
	19 Warm – Rain – 55°	18 30.1R, 24°, cldy occ. lt snow
	20 Cold front overnight. 22° at dawn. Some bare ground (first since 12/4/95) but still good snow cover.	19 30.2 S, 26°, cldy
		20 30.0 S, 30°, clear
	A possum crosses back yard at noon. Very few birds. No juncos, purples.	

January

Week 4

Weather _____

Outside
  Vegetables _____

Fruit _____

Flowers _____

Bulbs _____

Shrubs/Trees _____

Lawns _____

Greenhouse _____

Notes _____

Year *Cambridge* 1993

22

Titmouse begins
to sing.

28 Turned bitter
cold and
windy —
down to 10°
nights

31 3-4" snow

Juncos, white throat,
downy, mockingbird,
chickadees, fewer
Starlings (!). Cardinals,
titmice. Song sparrow.

Year *Newbury* 1994

22 Hit +20° for the first
time in a week

23 Two Red-Tails,
probably a pair,
at barn 107

24-25 Thaw.
Close to 40°

26 Snow overnight—
3", + bitter cold—
+5° by breakfast
Strong N + NE winds.
Redpolls back, also
goldfinch. Over 20
Purple Finch.

28 Heavy rain, warm,
over 40°

30 Turns cold again

31 10° at dawn

Spruce near house
taken down.

YEAR 1995

YEAR 1996

YEAR 1997

Generally
mild,
no snow

22 Dusting overnight.

23 Mild.
Cardinal sings

24 Rain, wind.
Most snow gone.

25 Cold, clear

26 10° at dawn

27 Mid-forties, near
gale SE, rain.

28 Mid-twenties, strong
N.W. Not much
snow left.

29 Cold. Birds return
>20 mourning doves,
numerous starlings.
Duct stayed over minutes.
← Squirrel building
nest in spruce.
Still few birds.

1996

29 Cooper's Hawk takes
mourning dove out of
flock of 20-plus
on back porch, eats
it in compost.

30 Snowing, 30° at
dawn. 1½"
Deer, skunk @
Plum Island.

31 Flurries in Am,
turns colder

29 Return.
Clear, cold,
N.W.-N.E
wind

30 Snow flurries
off the ocean
50 high.

31 More flurries.
A lot 1" in
all. 20°s

1998

21 30.1R, 28°, clear

23 30.8R, 18°, cldy
lt snow, gusty
}0.8"
}Ltg
}Fall

24 30.0S, 32° rain
25 29.6R, 30°, snow
becoming clear, sunny
26 29.9R, 25°, clear
27 30.8R, 12°, clear. Water
main break!

28 AWAY UNTIL 02/08

FEBRUARY

God Almighty first planted a garden;
and, indeed, it is the purest of human
pleasures.

FRANCIS BACON
ESSAYS, OF GARDENS

In the Garden
Bertha Wegmann

FEBRUARY

WEEK 1

Cavalick

YEAR _1993_

Newbury

YEAR _1994_

WEATHER _____

OUTSIDE
  VEGETABLES _____

1 Still bitter cold,
light snow.

Cold — about 10°
every night

FRUIT _____

2 8° at dawn.
Record low for
season so far.
light snow - "lake
effect"

4 golden-crowned
Kinglet.

FLOWERS _____

BULBS _____

1998

5 ⎫ Mild spell,
6 ⎬ lovely days,
    about freezing

SHRUBS/TREES _____

AWAY IN S. FLA
ALL WEEK

7 Turns cold again

LAWNS _____

GREENHOUSE _____

NOTES _____

YEAR 1995	YEAR 1996	YEAR 1997

1995

3 Cold - 8° in AM

4 Snow, strong winds S, Temp rises from 25 to close to 40, Rain.

5 Gusty NW winds, Back to 20° at dawn. Few Birds: Chick., P. Finch, 1 Junco, Mourning Doves

6 -4° at dawn. Blustery NW winds. High = 12°

7 -7° at dawn. MBR cold water line frozen! M's stuck. High = 15 or so Both mergansers at bridge, large rafty eiders at harbormouth.

1996

1 5° at dawn, clear, bright. Ailanthus cut! Hooray!

3 12° at dawn, 10° at 7:30. Light snow - 2-3" at most. 16° High

4 -2° at dawn. 8° High. Clear!

5 -18° at dawn. Clear. 15° High

6 +3° at dawn. Clear. 18° High

7 +2° at dawn, reaches 20's during day

Sun much stronger in E + S windows in AM, W in PM

1997

1 Cloudy, 20s, 1° overnight.

2 Mild — 28° at dawn, clear

3 Mostly cloudy, some clears,

4 occ. flurries, Upper 20s, Lower 30s

5 35° at dawn, rain over sleet, messy! Rain until mid-afternoon, occ. heavy.

6 32° at dawn, cloudy, clearing by mid-day, mild

7 22°, clear at dawn. Clouds over, leaden, new NE wind, 20s all day

Snowy owl (imm) on DS Island

FEBRUARY

WEEK 2

Cambridge
Newbury

YEAR 1993
YEAR 1994

WEATHER _____

OUTSIDE

VEGETABLES _____

8 ⎫
9 ⎬ milder,
  ⎬ above freezing
10 ⎭ days

8 Single numbers
all day, Lake-
effect snow
showers. Real
snow - 6" -
overnight

FRUIT _____

9 5° at 6 A.M.
light snow
continues
Carolina Wren at
feeder

FLOWERS _____

BULBS _____

SHRUBS/TREES _____

12 Snow turning
to rain,
Then freezing.

10 0° at 7:30AM

LAWNS _____

11 "Lake Effect" snow
in morning.
Sparrow Hawk.
Realstorm follows:
Another 6" on
no. Very light

GREENHOUSE _____

1998

8 Return. No new snow,
little seed eaten

NOTES _____

9 30.25 S, 20°, clear
10 30.45 R, 25°, clear
11 30.4 F, 34°, fog
12 29.5 F 45°, rain →
   ptly cldy, mild.
   WITCH HAZEL BLOOMS!

12 15° at 7:30
gorgeous morning.

13 minor ice/snow
showers.

13 29.6 R, 35°, clear

witch Hazel

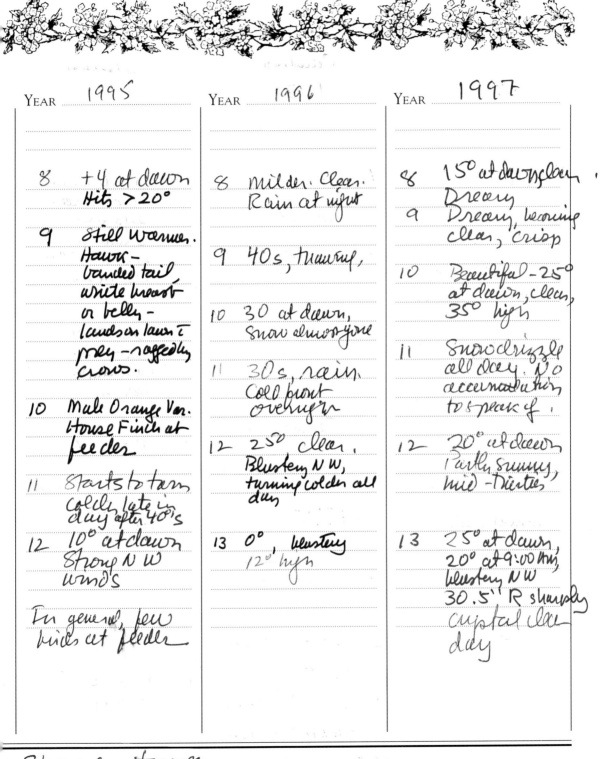

YEAR 1995	YEAR 1996	YEAR 1997

1995

8   +4 at dawn. Hits > 20°

9   Still warmer. Hawk — banded tail, white breast or belly — lands on lawn w/ prey — raggedly crows.

10   Male Orange Var. House Finch at feeder

11   Starts to turn colder late in day after 40's

12   10° at dawn. Strong N W winds

In general, few birds at feeder

1996

8   Milder. Clear. Rain at night

9   40s, thawing,

10   30 at dawn, Snow almost gone

11   30s, rain. Cold front overnight

12   25° clear. Blustery N W, turning colder all day

13   0°, blustery 12° high

1997

8   15° at dawn, clear. Dreary

9   Dreary, becoming clear, crisp

10   Beautiful - 25° at dawn, clear, 35° high

11   Snow/drizzle all day. No accumulation to speak of.

12   20° at dawn Partly sunny, mid-Thirties

13   25° at dawn, 20° at 9:00 AM, blustery N W 30.5" R sharply crystal clear day

Strong sun through E & S windows in morning now

FEBRUARY

Cambridge

Newburn

WEEK 3

WEATHER _____

OUTSIDE

   VEGETABLES _____

   FRUIT _____

   FLOWERS _____

   BULBS _____

   SHRUBS/TREES _____

   LAWNS _____

GREENHOUSE _____

NOTES _____

YEAR 1993

15 Snow again.
Very cold all
week.

Titmice starting
to sing

21 Snow. Robin.

1998
14 30.2R, 15°, clear, NW
breeze
15 30.5R, 5°, clear, quite N.
16 30.8R, 4°, clear, calm
17 30.2F, 34°, rain
18 Poured all day

21 Snow again.
Robin on
Contoaster
Attlis
19 29.7F, 35°, occ.
drizzle

20 29.8R, 34°, thin
o'cast. Barometer fell late

21 29.6R, 36°, cldy

YEAR 1994

14 Warming trend, mr
c'ast - result: 20s,
high wind, better

15 5° at 7:00 m.

19 Warm, sunny

20 Warm, sunny -
50s

21 Warm, cloudy,
showers

Few

Cardinal starts to sing.
Lovely witch hazel

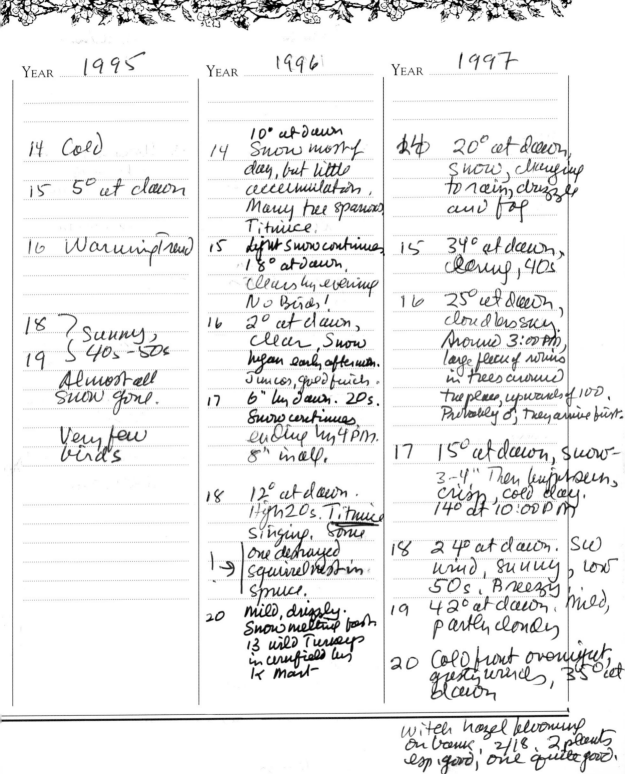

YEAR 1995	YEAR 1996	YEAR 1997
14 Cold	14 10° at dawn. Snow most of day, but little accumulation. Many tree sparrows, Titmice.	14 20° at dawn, snow, changing to rain, drizzle and fog
15 5° at dawn	15 light snow continues. 18° at dawn. Clears by evening. No Birds!	15 34° at dawn, clearing, 40s
16 Warming trend	16 2° at dawn, clear. Snow began early afternoon. Juncos, goldfinches.	16 25° at dawn, cloudless sky. Around 3:00 PM, large flock of ravens in trees around the place, upwards of 100. Probably ♂, they arrive first.
18 ⎱ Sunny, 19 ⎰ 40s-50s. Almost all snow gone. Very few birds	17 6" by dawn. 20s. Snow continues ending by 4 PM. 8" in all.	17 15° at dawn, snow 3-4" Then bright sun, crisp, cold day. 14° at 10:00 PM
	18 12° at dawn. High 20s. Titmice singing. Some	18 24° at dawn. SW wind, sunny, low 50s. Breezy
	1→ one destroyed squirrel nest in spruce.	19 42° at dawn. mild, partly cloudy
	20 mild, drizzly. Snow melting fast. 13 wild Turkeys in cornfield by K Mart.	20 Cold front overnight, gusty winds, 35° at dawn

Witch hazel blooming on bank, 2/18. 2 plants esp. good, one quite good.

FEBRUARY

WEEK 4

WEATHER _____

OUTSIDE

   VEGETABLES _____

   FRUIT _____

   FLOWERS _____

   BULBS _____

   SHRUBS/TREES _____

   LAWNS _____

GREENHOUSE _____

NOTES _____

Cambridge

YEAR 1993

22 6" heavy snow
topped by freezing
rain overnight.

Cardinal singing.
Chickadees
getting pink,
as are juncos'
bills.

23 2" new snow

Balance of month
cold & clear.

Cardinals begin
to sing.

1998
22 30.1 R, 36°, sunny, calm,
   hit 48°
23 30.3 R, 30°, cldy, damp
24 29.7 F, 34°, gale winds, heavy
   rain
25 29.5 R, 37°, cldy, drizzle
26 29.6 R, 35, clear
27 29.8 R, 35, o'cast
   crocus blooming on S. side
   of house. sunny, 50s
28 30.1 R, 30°, clear
   Shredded leaves

Newbury

YEAR 1994

22 Turning
colder — 40 in
AM, 20 by night

Cardinal singing

23 Snow — about
6" by dawn
on the 24th
then fine sleet.
Hordes of Purple &
Gold Finches when
snow begins. Also
the 2 tree sparrows

24 Skunk trotted
across lawn/snow
at 4:30 AM. Fine
sleet/freezing rain.
Nasty.
Red-Tail in evergreen
in Walsh's yard.

26 Another dose of snow —
dry, light.
Raccoon in Walsh
yard early afternoon

27 5° at dawn. Strong
winds.

Year 1995	Year 1996	Year 1997

1995

21 Mild, partly + sunny

24 Rain in AM Turned cold in afternoon + strong NW winds

25 Cold + windy — Under 30° all day

26 6° at dawn Birds back! Cardinal, Mourning Dove, P Finch singing

27 10° at dawn. Fine dry snow in AM. A few juncos, WB Nuthatch, Chickadees

28 Overnight snow & ice. ¼-½" on trees. Lots of birds.

1996

21 Fog, drizzle, rain. 40s

22 40 at dawn. Fog

23 Drizzly, mild, fog

24 Rain, drizzle, fog, mild. Clearing in afternoon

25 Blusterous NW wind — 40 mph or more, but still mild — 40s in AM

26 Windy, mild

27 Windy, mild, witch hazel begun to bloom on 02/26. Snow all gone except a few patches.

28 40 at dawn! Overcast. cold front in PM

29 20s all day blustery

Witch Hazel - Two plants particularly spectacular!

1997

21 35° at dawn, having warmed overnight. Ptly cloudy. To Newcastle

22 Returns. Warm (70°), breezy, cold front, squall mid-afternoon, then clearing

23 26° at dawn, clear. Cold, windy all day

24 24° at dawn, clear, gusty winds, low 30s 30.5"

25 10° at dawn, gusty overnight but no pressure change — 30.5"

26 27° at dawn, up 7° from 10:00 PM last night. Mild, sunny, SW winds. Baro ↓ 30.05

27 40° showers, fog, 29.8" Foggy, drizzle, 40s all day. 29.6" ↓

28 33°, pblycldy

Another Snowy Owl on P.I. Cardinal singing, also Titmouse

at Seddlesc

MARCH

For winter's rains and ruins are over,

And all the seasons of snows and sins;

The days dividing lover and lover,

The light that loses, the night that wins;

And in green underwood and cover

Blossom by blossom the spring begins.

CHARLES SWINBURNE
ATALANTA IN CALYDON

A Cottage Garden
James Matthews

MARCH

WEEK 1

WEATHER _____

OUTSIDE
   VEGETABLES _____

   FRUIT _____

   FLOWERS _____

   BULBS _____

   SHRUBS/TREES _____

   LAWNS _____

GREENHOUSE _____

NOTES _____

YEAR Cambridge 1993

1 Cold spell
   begins to
   break.

   Witch Hazel
   begins to bloom
             *

4-5 Wet snow,
     NE wind
     1995
1 29.9 F, 36°, drizzly
2. 29.75 F, 34°, clear after fog,
   warm
3. 29.6 F, 34°, fog, raw

4. 29.75 R 34° clear →
   ptly cldy, NW wind

5. 30.0 R, 34°, drizzle
6. AWAY
7.   "

YEAR Newbury 1994

1   10° at dawn,
    windy all day

2   5° at dawn
    but light winds.
    Temp. hasn't hit
    32° since 2/22

3. Snow. Strong NE wind
    changes to sleet.
    Back to snow
    overnight

5-7 Milder,
     thaw begins

     Imm. eagle,
     Iceland gull
     at lighthouse
     point

Shredded leaves,
transplanted vines
Primroses bloom
Grackles.

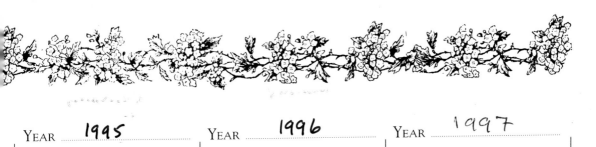

Year 1995	Year 1996	Year 1997

1995

1-3 Cold, partly cloudy. Very little melting. Ice damson roof.

Entire area is a "Crystal Palace" - gorgeous!

4 10° at dawn.

5 Moderating trend

1996

1 15 at 5:30 AM. Sunny, cold

2 25 at dawn, cloudy, snow on way

3 4-5" in all. Cold, blustery, 20s

4 Cold, blustery, crystal clear

5 18° at dawn 3" overnight

6 25° at dawn, snow off + on all day

7 25° at dawn, light snow falling.

One juncoat feeder; nothing else.

Tree work - clean up, pruning, culling

1997

1 Cloudy, cool

2 " "

3 32 at dawn, hazy sun, becoming cloudy

4 34 at dawn, cloudy, and so all day

5 Clear, warm sun, 40's in AM, becoming cloudy by evening

6 Rain overnight 40 at dawn, 29.25" ↓ from 30.5" high wind warnings. High winds from noon to 8:00 PM, when barometer ↑ to 29.65"

7 28°, 29.0" ↑ gales over, but still windy. Mid 30s for a high

No, Whisper, here for several years now

← Tundra Swan
Pintail
Thousands of Eider

Reducing herd on PI
Song sparrow sing in Nbpt

MARCH

WEEK 2

Cambridge

YEAR 1993

Newbury

YEAR 1994

WEATHER _____

OUTSIDE

   VEGETABLES _____

8 Snow, turning
to heavy rain,
loosing snow
cover.
4 immature (bald)
eagles at bridge

   FRUIT _____

   FLOWERS _____

   BULBS _____

12 With Hazel in
full bloom

10 mild, clearing
begins

11 mild, Flicker
at suet feeder

   SHRUBS/TREES _____

13 Blizzard.
±17" snow

12 Colder - 18° at
dawn

   LAWNS _____

GREENHOUSE _____

14 Snow squalls,
Turning cold.

1995

8 Return. 30.3 F
9 30.1 F, 34°, Rain
10 - 15 AWAY

14 Mild spell begins

NOTES _____

Saw first woodchuck
this week

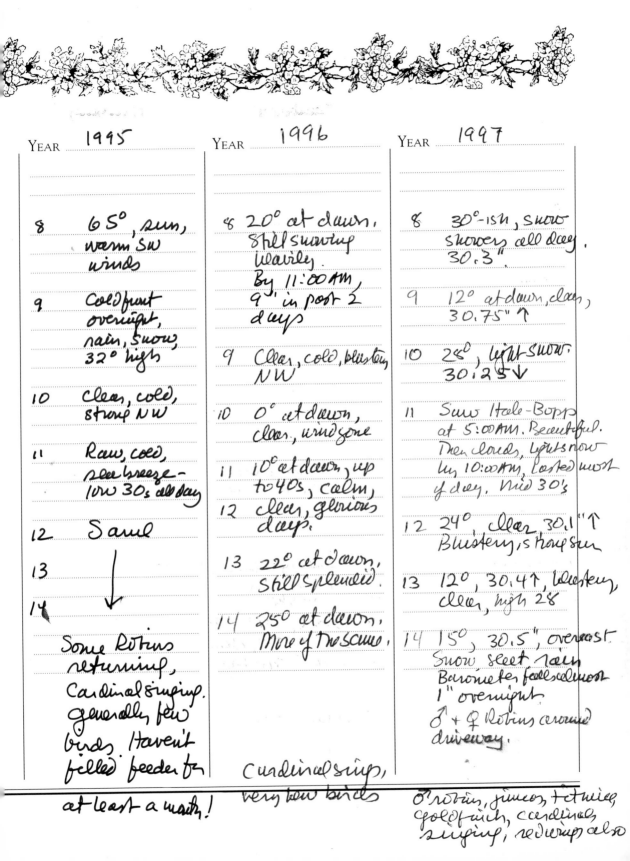

YEAR 1995	YEAR 1996	YEAR 1997

1995

8   65°, sun, warm SW winds

9   Cold front overnight, rain, snow 32° highs

10   Clear, cold, strong NW

11   Raw, cold, sleet breeze – low 30s all day

12   Same

13

14

Some Robins returning. Cardinal singing. generally few birds. Haven't filled feeder for at least a month!

1996

8   20° at dawn. Still snowing lightly. By 11:00 AM, 9" in past 2 days

9   Clear, cold, blustery NW

10   0° at dawn, clear, wind gone

11   10° at dawn, up to 40s, calm,

12   clear, glorious day.

13   22° at dawn, still splendid.

14   25° at dawn. More of the same.

Cardinal sings, very few birds

1997

8   30°-ish, snow showers all day. 30.3"

9   12° at dawn, clear, 30.75" ↑

10   28°, light snow. 30.25 ↓

11   Saw Hale-Bopp at 5:00 AM. Beautiful. Then clouds, light snow by 10:00 AM, lasted most of day. Mid 30's

12   24°, clear 30.1" ↑ Blustery, strong sun

13   12°, 30.4 ↑, blustery, clear, high 28

14   15°, 30.5", overcast. Snow sleet rain Barometer falls almost 1" overnight ♂ + ♀ Robins around driveway.

♂ robins, juncos, titmice, goldfinch, cardinals, singing, redwings also

MARCH

WEEK 3

WEATHER _____

OUTSIDE

  VEGETABLES _____

  FRUIT _____

  FLOWERS _____

  BULBS _____

  SHRUBS/TREES _____

  LAWNS _____

GREENHOUSE _____

NOTES _____

YEAR _Cambridge_ _1993_

15 7° at dawn!

17 50°! Rain.
Mourning doves
singing.
Many white-
Throats.

18 3" snow
overnight.
15° in AM.
Cardinal sings.
Robin seems to be
staking claim to
fountain + large
holly.

_1998_
15 Snow showers
16 30.5R, 24°, clear
17 30.8R, 20°, clear
18 30.6F, 26°, hazy
    o'cast, rain incoming
19 30.3F 35, rain, NE
    winds.
20 30's, cldy, but dry
21 30.1S 29, lt snow,
    strong NE winds all
    day + night

YEAR _Newbury_ _1994_

15 Sunny, 40-ish
16 damp, much
    melting

17 Snow overnight,
    turning colder.
    2 Redwings at
    feeder

21 Warm, sunny,
    first day to feel
    like Spring

Set trap this
week. Junipers moved

YEAR 1995	YEAR 1996	YEAR 1997
15 Cloudy, drizzly, cool	15 Mild, drizzly. Birds — juncos, cardinal, chick., WB Nut, Downy, Grackle in WB pt.	15 34°, 29.7"↑, ptly cldy ⇒ clear, blustery. 8° ↑↑ Robins still here.
16 Same		16 20°, 30.25↑, clear, windy
17 Same	16 25° at dawn, blustery, lots of juncos. Redwing, Grackles	17 14°, 30.50↑, clear, calm
18 Same until mid-morning. SUN!	17 22°. Sunny, up to 50°	18 34°, clear, breezy, 30's
19 Sunny, 40s	18 A ROBIN !! From 25° to 50°.	19 18°, clear, calm, 30.50↑ warms to upper 30's, strong sun
20 Sunny, 40s		20 30°, 30"↓ overcast ⇒ clear, lt SE breeze, becoming overcast, drizzly snow showers.
Very few robins. Where are they?	19 Mild becoming warm. Rain, thunder, overnight	21 25°, 29.8"↑, clear
Started clean-up of garden on 19th.	20 Clouds, sun, sprinkles, cool	22 34°, 29.4" drizzly becoming ptly cldy, gusty NW
	21 Same	
	Saw Gt Gray Owl in Rowley at last.	Grackles back, migrating ospreys, TVs

MARCH

WEEK 4

Cambridge

YEAR 1993

Newbury
1994

YEAR

WEATHER _____

OUTSIDE

VEGETABLES _____

22 8" heavy wet snow

22 ROBIN!
Heavy, cold rain

FRUIT _____

23 Thaw begins

23-24 Warm,
spring-like.
20 or so
redwings on
lawn.

FLOWERS _____

1995

BULBS _____

22 29.5+S, snow,
gusty NE, 26°
snow/drizzle, all day

Woodchuck
exploring!

SHRUBS/TREES _____

23 29.8R, 26°, clear,
calm, warming to
low 40s

LAWNS _____

24 32.0R, 25°, clear

GREENHOUSE _____

25 30.7R, 25° clear
ROBIN IN YARD
Warm

26 Warm

27 30.1F, 45°, ptly
cldy, Al most 80°!
8 top path up hill
clone. Water turned
on. Remove hay.

NOTES _____

28 30.0SS, 55°, o'cast-
train. 80s, gusty SW

29 29.8S, 55°, clear, calm,
80s

30 DITTO

31 90°! NO BLUEBIRDS

ROBINS SING. ALSO
Juncos trilling. BLUE-
BIRDS! House hunting @ Regina's + here. 3/27-30. 3/31: gone!

Forsythia begins,
shrubs leafing
out. Arnus Mes.
Golden cr. Kinglet

1995	1996	1997
21 Spring-like, warm, sun, showers	22 Same	23 Clear, 20°, 29.9"↑ breezy
	23 Clear at dawn, 26°	24 Clear, 16°, 30.4↑, blustery
24 Turns colder. Snow flurries	24 Same.	25 Clear, 20°, 30.7↑ becoming cloudy, raw
25 Clear, cold	25 Warmer	
	26 48° at dawn, showers overnight 60s for high.	26 Cloudy, rain, 29.65 rain, 40°, becoming clear,
	27 Cold front over night – 24° at dawn gusty NW	27 30°, 29.9↑, clear, calm
	28 20° at dawn. Clear, calm.	28 30°, 30.1↑, clear, calm, bright comet at dawn. Crocus in bloom on top of ridge. Bulbs poking through. Forsythia about to bloom.
	29 25° at dawn, 30s all day, windy.	
	30 25° at dawn. Clear, windy, 40s	29 40°, 30.0↓ overcast, some fog. Heavy PM showers
Song Sparrow, juncos, mocking-bird, finch, gold + purple, a few robins, grackles & starlings, W. B. Nuthatches.	31 OUT LIKE A LAMB. 60, light breeze. Hyakutake – tail visible 1:30 AM 03/25 3:30 AM 03/27 Robin on front lawn, 03/26.	30 40°, 29.65, clearing, warming to 60s, NW breezes
	The work continues, started clean-up on 28th.	31 40° 29.75 S, drizzly, Temp drops, blizzard
		Removed hay from beds, ground workable.

APRIL

Awake, the land is scattered with light,
and see,

Uncanopied sleep is flying from field
and tree:

And blossoming boughs of April in laughter
shake.

ROBERT BRIDGES
AWAKE, MY HEART, TO BE LOVED

A Cottage Garden
G.H. Hughes

APRIL

WEEK 1

WEATHER _____

OUTSIDE

  VEGETABLES _____

  FRUIT _____

  FLOWERS _____

  BULBS _____

  SHRUBS/TREES _____

  LAWNS _____

GREENHOUSE _____

NOTES _____

YEAR — Cambridge 1993

Cool and damp, W75 of rain.

Everything is late

1998
1 42°, 30.2 R, cldy, quiet, NE, back door cold front & rain
2. 38° drizzly + rain all day
3 40°, 29.9 F, clear, calm → ptly cldy, a few sprinkles
4 36°, 29.8 R, nightrain 6° cast

5-6 Dreary NE, 39.75, 38-42°, dreary.

7 29.75 R, 36°, clear, warm — 60-154, breezy

YEAR — Newbury 1994

SPRING!
Uncovered Rhodos from mulch, fertilized + limed lawn, cleared woods, attacked bitter-sweet.

5   Work on stonewall begins

Antique Pearl
April Snow, Pink Diamond, Star Mag.,
daffs under LR S. window
Witch Hazel done

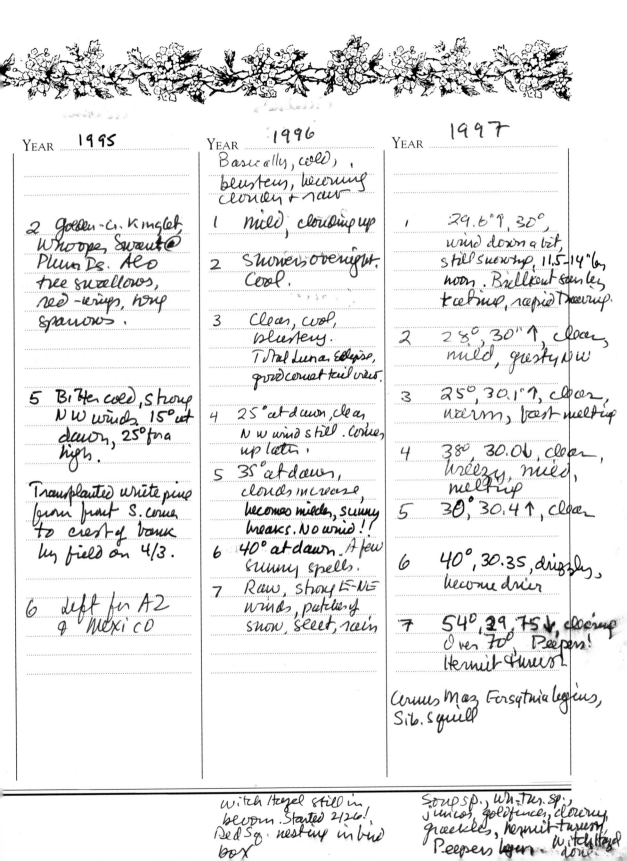

YEAR 1995	YEAR 1996	YEAR 1997
	Basically, cold, blustery, becoming cloudy + raw	
2 golden-cr. Kinglet. Whooper Swan @ Plum Dr. Also tree swallows, red-wings, house sparrows.	1 Mild, clouding up	1 29.6"↑, 30°, wind down a bit, still snowing, 11.5-14" by noon. Brilliant sun by teatime, rapid thawing.
	2 Showers overnight. Cool.	2 28°, 30"↑, clear, mild, gusty NW
	3 Clear, cool, blustery. Total Lunar Eclipse, good comet tail view.	3 25°, 30.1"↑, clear, warm, fast melting
5 Bitter cold, strong NW winds. 15° at dawn, 25° for a high.	4 25° at dawn, clear NW wind still. Comes up later.	4 38°, 30.0↓, clear, breezy, mild, melting
	5 35° at dawn, clouds increase, becomes milder, sunny breaks. No wind!!	5 30°, 30.4↑, clear
Transplanted white pine from front S. corner to crest of bank by field on 4/3.	6 40° at dawn. A few sunny spells.	6 40°, 30.35, drizzly, become drier
	7 Raw, strong E-NE winds, patchy snow, sleet, rain	7 54°, 29.75↓, clearing. Over 70°! Peepers! Hermit thrush
6 Left for AZ & Mexico		Cornus Mas Forsythia begins, Sib. squill

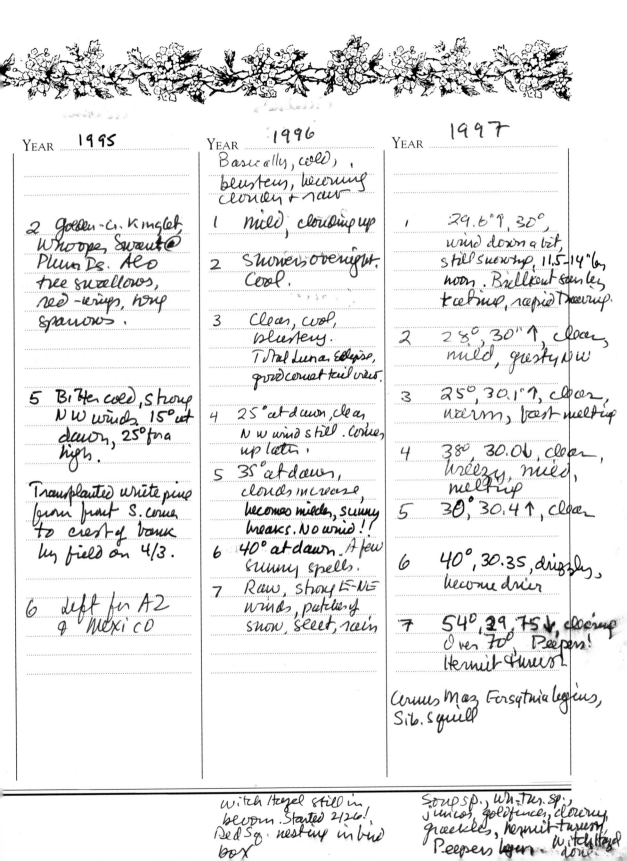
Witch Hazel still in bloom. Started 2/26! Red Sq. nesting in bird box

Song sp., Wh-thr. sp., Juncos, goldfinches, downy, grackles, hermit thrush, Peepers begun. Witch Hazel done

APRIL

WEEK 2

Cambridge

YEAR __1993__

Newbury
1994

YEAR ____

WEATHER _____

OUTSIDE

VEGETABLES _____

FRUIT _____

FLOWERS _____

BULBS _____

SHRUBS/TREES _____

LAWNS _____

GREENHOUSE _____

NOTES _____

1993 column:

Cool and
damp.

Cornus Mas
blooming.
Star Mag. just
budding.

R. Dauricum starting

14: Applied
Halts for
Crabgrass

_____

1998

8 30, OR, 30°, clear,
pleasant day.
Cedar Waxwing.
Weeping Cherry lovely.
9 AWAY UNTIL
25TH - GALAPA-
GOS

1994 column:

9 Chipping sparrow
at feeder.

Pair of song sparrows
in brush (?) and
composter.

Maples along drive
beginning to bud.
Poplar leafing out.

10 ♂ & ♀ Robins
on lawn.

11-12 Made and
planted Rhodo
nursery bed.

Put up bird houses.
Chicks investigate one
immediately.

13 Possum strolls
across lawn.
R. Dauricum starting

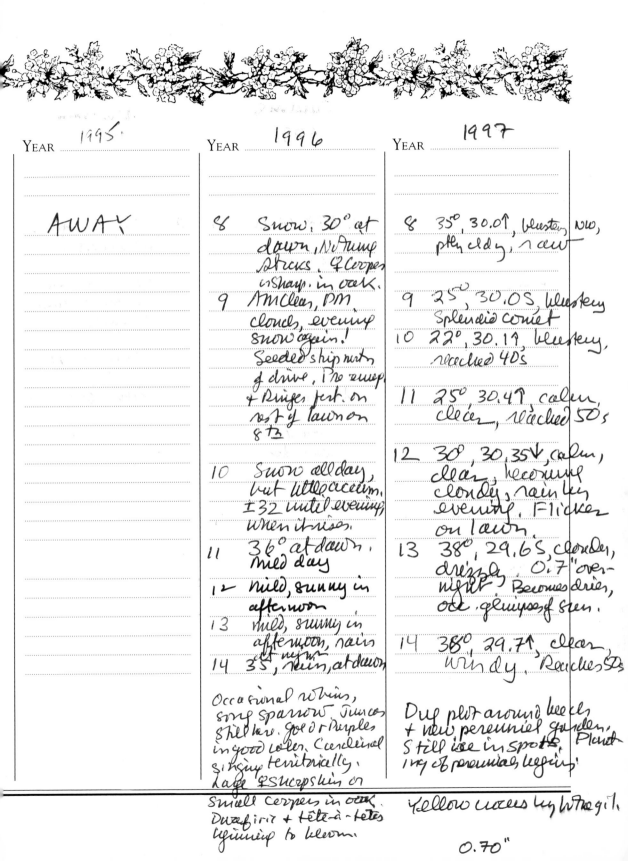

YEAR 1995	YEAR 1996	YEAR 1997
AWAY	8 Snow, 30° at dawn. Nothing sticks. 4 Creepers in shape. in oak.	8 35°, 30.0↑, blustery, NW, ptly cldy, raw
	9 AM Clear, PM clouds, evening snow again! Seeded ship nurt of drive. Tho creep + Binges just on rest of lawn on 8+9	9 25°, 30.0S, blustery Splendid comet
		10 22°, 30.1↑, blustery, reached 40s
		11 25°, 30.4↑ calm, clear, reached 50s
	10 Snow all day, but little accum. I 32 until evening, when it rises.	12 30°, 30.35↓, calm, clear, becoming cloudy, rain by evening. Flicker on lawn.
	11 36° at dawn, mild day	13 38°, 29.6S, cloudy, drizzle, 0.7" overnight. Becomes drier, occ. glimpses of sun.
	12 mild, sunny in afternoon	
	13 mild, sunny in afternoon, rains at night	14 38°, 29.7↑, clear windy. Reaches 50s
	14 35, rain, at dawn	

Occasional robins, song sparrow. Juncos still here. Gold & Purples in good color. Cardinal singing territorially. Large & sharpskin or small creepers in oak. Dwarf iris + tête-à-têtes beginning to bloom.

Dug plot around beech + new perennial garden. Still ice in spots. Planting of perennials begins.

Yellow crocus by the gill.

0.70"

APRIL

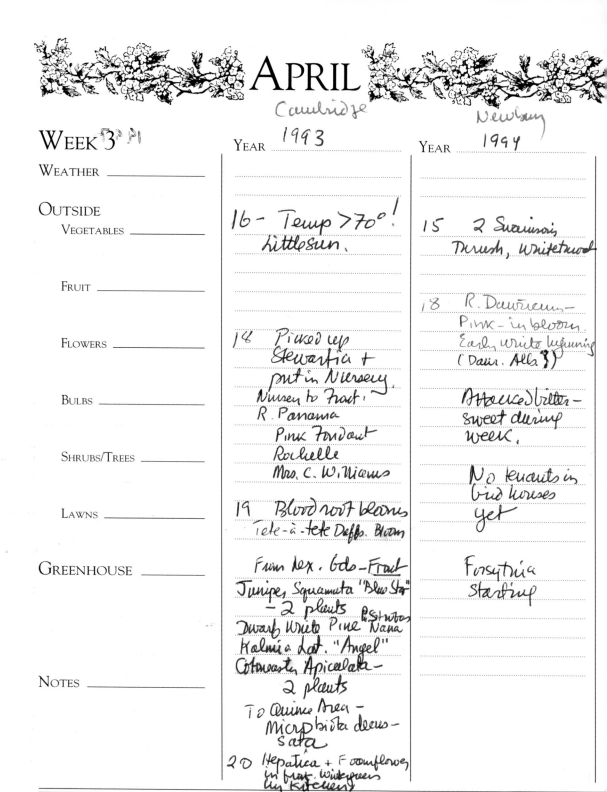

Cambridge

WEEK 3ʳᵈ PI

YEAR 1993

Newbury

YEAR 1994

WEATHER _____

OUTSIDE

VEGETABLES _____

16 - Temp >70°!
Little sun.

15   2 Swainson's
Thrush, Whitethroat

FRUIT _____

18   R. Dauricum -
Pink - in bloom.
Early white beginning
(Dauir. Alba?)

FLOWERS _____

18   Picked up
Stewartia +
put in Nursery.
Nursery to Frost.
R. Panama
Pink Fondant
Rochelle
Mrs. C. Williams

BULBS _____

Attacked bitter-
sweet during
week.

SHRUBS/TREES _____

No tenants in
bird houses
yet

LAWNS _____

19   Blood root blooms
Tête-à-tete Daffs. Bloom

GREENHOUSE _____

From Dex. Gdo - Frost
Juniper Squamata "Blue Star"
- 2 plants P. Strobus
Dwarf White Pine 'Nana'
Kalmia Lat. "Angel"
Cotoneaster Apiculata -
2 plants

Forsythia
starting

NOTES _____

To Quince Area -
Microbiota decus-
sata
20 Hepatica + Foamflower
in bud. Wintergreen
in kitchen?

Erica × Darleyensis,
pink + white, in
Quince Area

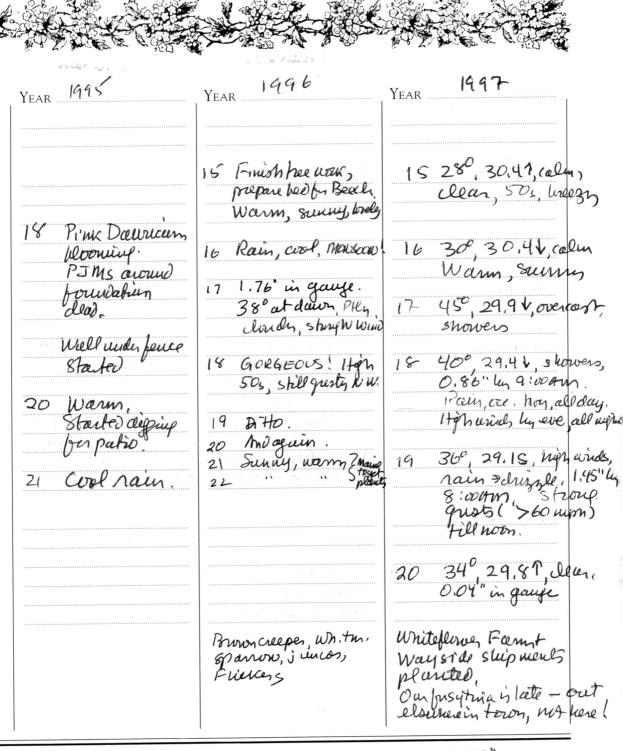

Year 1995	Year 1996	Year 1997

1995

18 Pink Daurican blooming. PJMs around foundation dead.

Well under fence started

20 Warm. Started digging for patio.

21 Cool rain.

1996

15 Finish tree work, prepare bed for Beach. Warm, sunny, lovely

16 Rain, cool, Moscow!

17 1.76" in gauge. 38° at dawn, PH, cloudy, strong W wind

18 GORGEOUS! High 50s, still gusty N.W.

19 Ditto.
20 And again.
21 Sunny, warm } Maine tour plants
22   "   " }

Brown creeper, Wh. tm. sparrow, juncos, Flickers

1997

15 28°, 30.4↑, calm, clear, 50s, breezy

16 30°, 30.4↓ calm Warm, sunny

17 45°, 29.9↓, overcast, showers

18 40°, 29.4↓, showers, 0.86" by 9:00am. Rain, occ. hvy, all day. High winds by eve, all night

19 36°, 29.1S, high winds, rain → drizzle, 1.45" by 8:00am. Strong gusts (>60 mph) till noon.

20 34°, 29.8↑, clear, 0.04" in gauge

Whiteflower Farm & Wayside shipments planted. Our forsythia is late — out elsewhere in town, not here!

1.76"

2.35"

APRIL

WEEK 4

Cambridge
YEAR 1993

Newbury
1994

WEATHER Warm, breezy, mostly sunny, some showers

Cool, very dry, week

OUTSIDE

VEGETABLES _____

21 R. Pink Diamond (Hill) and Early White (Quince) start to bloom.
Forsythia starts.

22 28° at dawn

FRUIT _____

Wall complete. Transplanted 4 Cotoneaster to bank above wall, R. Pink Diamond

FLOWERS _____

23 35° at dawn

BULBS _____

Alternate warm/cool for balance of week

SHRUBS/TREES _____

24 Malta (Hill) starts

28 Parker River, Kayaking? Snowy Egret, Gr. Heron, Kingfisher, Harriers, Gr. Yellowlegs

LAWNS _____

25 R. April Snow (Hill) starts

26 Turns colder,
GREENHOUSE _____
rainy

Dan. Alb. x Carol.

27

28 ~~R. Pink Diamond~~
Mary Fleming
Malta

27 SNOW! Just a trace.

29 Cool, Cloudy

NOTES _____

30 Hordes y yellowlegs, also Great Egret, P. Martin
Moved arborvitae to screen composter

4/30 Sharpshinned Hawk dive bombs white-throats at potvergillas, without success.

YEAR 1995	YEAR 1996	YEAR 1997

1995

28 Patio completed. Also stonewall under fence.

Lots of robins, white-throats.

0.1" rain

29 Yellow-rumped warblers.

Cool, a few sprinkles.

Pink Diamond,

Mary Fleming, White Daviricum, Forsythia starting.

See → also
1998
04/21 Cherry finished
Magnolia - full
Pink Dia. - fading
Arctic Pearl - full → fading
April Snow - full
← Malta - full
Shad - one in bloom
Mary Fleming - full

1996

2.64" rain + some snow

23 Thunderstorms overnight - 0.8" rain. Warm, sunny. Much planting - 3 Fothergillas, 3 R. Alb. Elegens. Beginning: Pink Diamond, Wh. Daviricum, Arctic Pearl Cornus Mas in bloom. Mag. Stellata.

24 Cool, windy 0.08"
25 Planted elms
26 Magnolia, Forsythia gusty SW, warm
27 50 at dawn. Showers overnight < .05"

Warm, sunny Malta begins.
28 32° at dawn. Sunny. 2 flickers displaying
29 Rain. Robin building in Juniper
30 0.75"
Splendid chirping sp. on 28th. White Throats & Juncos gone by 28th.
No - 1 Wispy white Throats on 29th
Robins nesting in Juniper again.

1997

21 40°, 29.81, high thin broken, becoming clear, warm

22 35, 29.95

AWAY

24 Return PM
0.82" in gauge
Blooming: Cherry, Wh. Daviricum, Magnolia, Pink Diamond, Mary Fleming, Early White (= Daviricum?) PJM, Shad Bean
30 35°, 30"↑, Clearer Hit 70!

← See Also 1998
20-25 0.9", mild]
26 Cool
27 30, 1", 38°
28 30&3"R, 35° Fair
Cutting Daffs, full bloom
Spellbinder
→ Magnolias finished
Laurie beginning
Arctic Pearl finishing
PJM

MAY

Oh, Adam was a gardener, and God who

made him sees

That half a proper gardener's work is done

upon his knees,

So when your work is finished, you can

wash your hands and pray

For the Glory of the Garden, that it may

not pass away!

RUDYARD KIPLING
THE GLORY OF THE GARDEN

Abbey Leix, Eire
Ernest Arthur Rowe

MAY

WEEK 1 PP1

WEATHER _____

OUTSIDE
   VEGETABLES _____

   FRUIT _____

   FLOWERS _____

   BULBS _____

   SHRUBS/TREES _____

   LAWNS _____

GREENHOUSE _____

NOTES _____

YEAR 1993

Maine from
now until fall.

1998
1 Hazy sun, warm
Saw woodchuck. Fewer [?]
2 50°, 29.7 F, lt rain,
NE breeze "0.70"
becoming sunny
3. 50°, 29.7 R, fog, cool
4 50, 30.1 R, fog, cool
5 " " " , cool
6 " " " , rain, cool
1.1" overnight

7 " " " rain, cool
0.6" overnight

5/6 - Planting Day:
Birch clump,
Red Oak,
Weeping Hemlock
Moved Stewartia.

2.4" rain

YEAR 1994.

1 Cool, .5" rain

2-3 Side fence in.

3 Trees arrive.
R. kiskei starts.
1 t. Zarloutad + 2
Can. Hemlock to
shield shed + work
area, also 2
Austrian Pine (P.
Nigra Austriaca)
John begins.

4 4 Pinus Albi...
4 R. Maxonun
3 "Magnifica"
1 Ilex pedunculosa +
1 male

3 white Pines
3 red Pines

5 Rain, cool. 1.2"

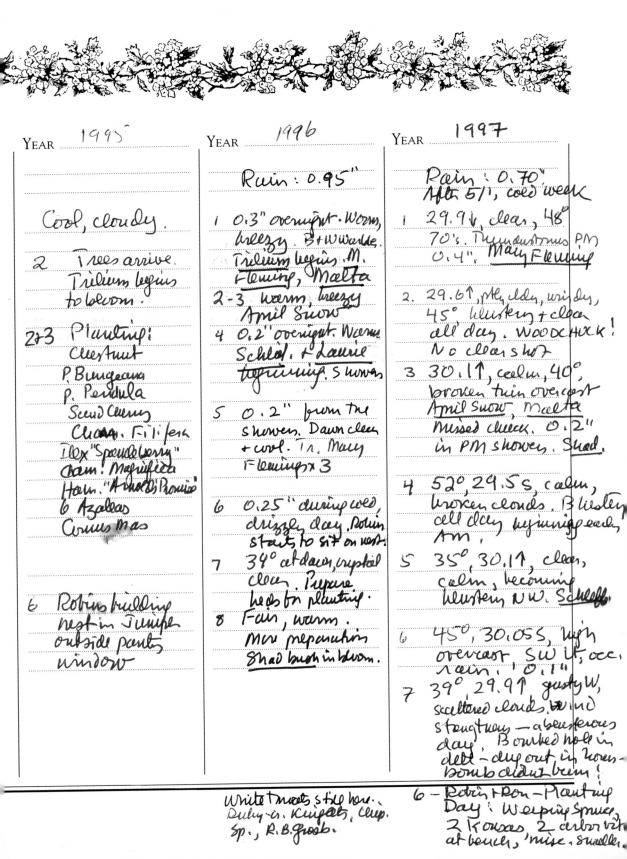

YEAR 1995	YEAR 1996	YEAR 1997

YEAR 1995

Cool, cloudy.

2 Trees arrive.
Trilium begins
to bloom.

2+3 Planting:
Chestnut
P. Bungeana
P. Pendula
Scud Cherry
Cham. Fili/era
Ilex "Spreadberry"
cham! Magnifica
Ham. "Arnold's Promise"
6 Azaleas
Cornus Mas

6 Robins building
nest in Juniper
outside pants
window

YEAR 1996

Rain : 0.95"

1 0.3" overnight. Warm,
breezy. B+W Warble.
Trilium begins. M.
Fleming, Malta

2-3 Warm, breezy
April Snow

4 0.2" overnight. Warm
Schled. + Laurie
beginning. Showers

5 0.2" from the
showers. Dawn clear
+ cool. In Mary
Flemings x 3

6 0.25" during cold,
drizzly day. Robin
starts to sit on nest.

7 39° at dawn, crystal
clear. Prepare
beds for planting.

8 Fair, warm.
More preparations
Shad bush in bloom.

YEAR 1997

Rain : 0.70"
After 5/1, cold week

1 29.9↓, clear, 48°
70's. Thunderstorms PM
0.4". Mary Fleming

2. 29.6↑, ptly cldy, windy,
45° blustery + clear
all day. WOODCHUCK!
No clear shot

3 30.1↑, calm, 40°,
broken thin overcast
April Snow, Malta
Missed check. 0.2"
in PM showers. Shad.

4 52°, 29.5 S, calm,
broken clouds. Blustery
all day by midnight early
AM.

5 35°, 30.1↑, clear,
calm, becoming
blustery NW. Schleff.

6 45°, 30.05 S, high
overcast. SW lt, occ.
rain. 0.1"

7 39°, 29.9↑ gusty W,
scattered clouds, wind
strengthen — a boisterous
day. Bombed hole in
dell — dug out in hours —
bomb didn't bloom!

6 - Robin + Ron - Planting
Day : Weeping Spruce,
2 Kousas, 2 arbor vit
at bench, misc. smalls,

MAY

WEEK 2 F PM

YEAR **1998** YEAR **1994**

WEATHER _____

OUTSIDE

VEGETABLES _____

8 50°, 30.0" S, fog, drizzly, cool. Glimpse of dim sun in PM

8 1.3" rain, R. Fairy, Mary, Bush, Malta

FRUIT _____

9 Same, raw SE, showers

10 1 rain, 2 Ilex Blue Princess from NE. R. Nodding Bells, Scarlet Wonder, beginning. Also Schlippenbachii J. de Perez.

FLOWERS _____

10 Same, raw, gusty NE, showers 0.70"

BULBS _____

11 Same 0.80"

House Wrens in woodpile near Harris's fence

SHRUBS/TREES _____

LAWNS _____

12 SUN AT DAWN - First since 5/2 30.2 R, 44°, gusty NE

12 Yellowthroat, pr. mincing birds, pr (?) Catbirds White cr. sparrow

GREENHOUSE _____

13 30.4 S, 40°, o'cast @ dawn → clear, breezy, cool

NOTES _____

14 30.4 S, 34°, clear, sunny, cool NE'

14 Warm, sunny. No rain since 5/8

1.5" rain

Planting + Transplanting

YEAR 1995	YEAR 1996	YEAR 1997
		Everything 1-2 weeks behind.
	Rain: 0.90"	Rain: 0.46"

1995

7 Chipping Sparrow at feeder

Dry

10 Planting: Dogwoods, Magnolias, Weeping Crab, Scintillation, etc.

11 Hard drizzle. Cold — 40s, E wind. Shadbush on wall in bloom.

12 1" in rain gauge. 1 egg in nest

14 Mild. Crow around, raggedy mockingbird pair. Robins spooked, but ♀ returns to nest.

1996

9 Cloudy, cool, occ. sunny breaks. Manure - 2 y composted, 2 y horse.

10 Light rain, cool. Pr. Wood Ducks in tree outside Bath! To Maine

11 Rain, cool. 0.45" on return in evening. No one on nest -!!

12 0.45" overnight. Drizzly, cool. Nest vacant. Another 0.24", 2 eggs left in nest.

13 Cool, clear, breezy

14 32° at clearing. Up to 60°! Brisk NW. Nodding Bells begins

Parula, Yellowthroat, Ovenbird, Towhee, Magnolia. At least 4 Orioles in Kriesberg, Sharp-tailed Sparrow

Bl.-tu. Blue, Hermit Thrush, Yellow-rump, Wh.-Cr. Sparrow outside. Black Throat Green

1997

8 38°, 30.0↑, clear, 4 NW, reaches 60s, brilliant day. Transplanted rhod.

9 44°, 30.1 S, thin overcast. Wren, swifts returned, robins, titmice paired. Drizzle all day

10 42°, 29.6↓, overcast. Only 0.06" in gauge—seems like full-day soaking drizzle. Drizzly all day again, cool.

11 40°, 29.6↑, ptly cldy. 0.10" in gauge. Receding clouds, mild, breezy. Heard oriole. Tr. Rhodos.

12 50°, 29.8↑, ptly cldy → clear, warm, 70s

13 50°, 29.75 R, thin overcast, threatened rain fizzles, sunny periods. Nodding Bells, Fairy Mary

14 48° 29.75 S, 0.3" overnight, broken clouds. Sprayed pines for caterpillars

M. found robins nesting in Can. Hemlock at top of dell. Oriole, Veery in yard

MAY

WEEK 3

WEATHER _____

OUTSIDE

VEGETABLES _____

FRUIT _____

FLOWERS _____

BULBS _____

SHRUBS/TREES _____

LAWNS _____

GREENHOUSE _____

NOTES _____

YEAR 1998

15 30.2↓, 38°, clear
   warm, lt breeze
   Swifts, Oriole

16 30.1S, 50°, clear,
   warm, sea breeze

17 30.2R, 50°, clear

18 30.1S, 50°, clear
   80°

19 Clear, cool
20 ?
21 29.9S, 48°, clear
   Dry cold front in
   late afternoon

21 29.6R, 45°, clear

Moved old composter back,
enlarging work area.
Transplanted nursery
rhododendrons.
Swallows investigate
house.

YEAR 1994

15 Warm, dry.
   Kingbirds, Oriole
   Mag. warbler, at
   least 2 others.

16 Northeaster. 1.1"
   rain, cool.
17 Same. Another 0.15"
18. Same. Another 0.05"
19. Same. Another 0.03"

20) Planted 6 R.
21) Dauricum album
   "Arctic Pearl" in
   front.
   Bl. Th. Green warbler

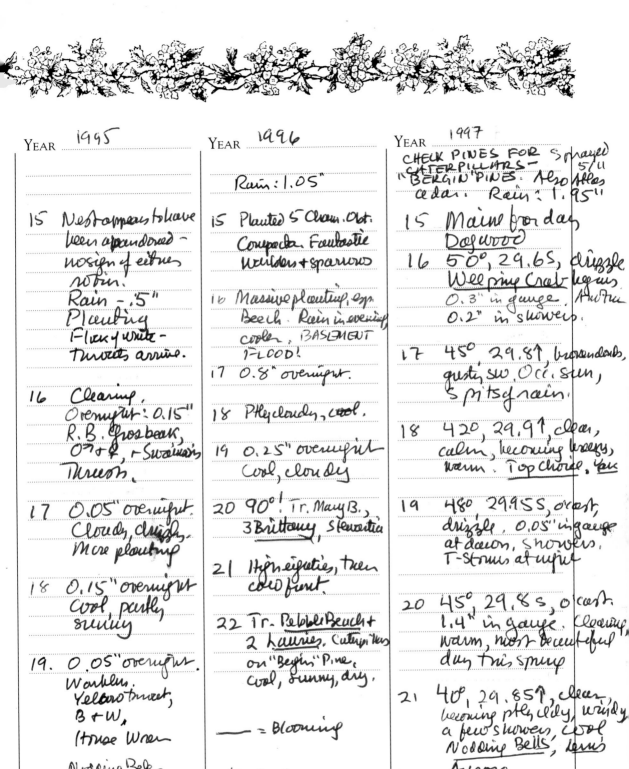

YEAR 1995	YEAR 1996	YEAR 1997

CHELK PINES FOR Sprayed
"CATERPILLARS - 5/11
"BERGIN" PINES. Also Atlas
cedar. Rain: 1.95"

Rain: 1.05"

1995

15 Nest appears to have
been abandoned -
no sign of either
robin.
Rain - .5"
Planting
Flock y white -
Throats arrive.

16 Clearing.
Overnight: 0.15"
R. B. Grosbeak,
♂ + ♀, - Swainson's
Thrush.

17 0.05" overnight.
Cloudy, drizzly,
More planting

18 0.15" overnight
Cool, partly
sunny

19. 0.05" overnight.
Warblers.
Yellow throat,
B + W,
House Wren

Nodding Bells
Laurie

America
Cataw. Album

1996

15 Planted 5 Cham. Obt.
Compacta. Fantastic
Warblers + sparrows

16 Massive planting, esp.
Beech. Rain in evening
cooler. BASEMENT
FLOOD!

17 0.8" overnight.

18 Ptly cloudy, cool.

19 0.25" overnight
Cool, cloudy

20 90°! Tr. Mary B.,
3 Brittany, Stewartia

21 High eighties, then
cold front.

22 Tr. Pebble Beach +
2 Lauries. Caterpillars
on "Bergin" Pine.
Cool, sunny, dry.

—— = Blooming

Lincoln's Sparrow

Rabbit.
Oriole(s)
Blackburnian (?)

1997

15 Maine for day.
Dogwood

16 50°, 29.65, drizzle
Weeping Crab begins
0.3" in gauge. Another
0.2" in showers.

17 45°, 29.8↑ broken clouds,
gusty, SW. Occ. sun,
5 spits of rain.

18 42°, 29.91, clear,
calm, becoming breezy,
warm. Top Choice. Yaw

19 48° 29.95 S, o'cast,
drizzle, 0.05" in gauge
at dawn, showers.
T-storms at night

20 45°, 29.8 S, o'cast.
1.4" in gauge. Clearing,
warm, most beautiful
day this spring

21 40°, 29.85↑, clear,
becoming ptly cld'y, windy
a few showers, cool.
Nodding Bells, Fern's
Aurora

Weeping White Pine
shows no growth -
needles pale.

MAY

WEEK 4

WEATHER _____

OUTSIDE

   VEGETABLES _____

   FRUIT _____

   FLOWERS _____

   BULBS _____

   SHRUBS/TREES _____

   LAWNS _____

GREENHOUSE _____

NOTES _____

YEAR _1994_

22 Warmest day so far —
well over 70°.
Oriole, Tanager,
Mystery warbler

23-30 Away in Round Pond.
0.4" in gauge on
return. R, Yak,
Mary Belle
in bloom.

31 From Cambridge:
2 Lauries
1 Fortunei (Mel. x
Gable)
2 Heather
1 Microbiota decus-
sata
1 Leucitue "Scarlatta"
Va. Bluebells
All planted 5/31 +
6/1
1 Weeping Blue
Spruce for ME

4.73"

YEAR _1995_

24 9/10" rain

25 Tree full of
yellow warblers

Yellow ladyslippers,
Sol. seal

29 .15" overnight

Yak, Pebble Beach,
Percy Wiseman
Laurie, Lem's
Aurora, Duance
"7 p Choice, Az.
"Sea breeze",
Cabalga x Pausey, Pink
Rochelle,
Mary Belle,
Stuart #18,
Az. "Naidris Evergreen"

30 0.1" overnight
P. Finch - 3 fledglings
Sprayed Poison Ivy

2.15"

2 Wood ducks in May

YEAR 1996	YEAR 1987	YEAR 1998
Rain = .42"		
	Rain = 0.4"	
	Month = 2.51"	
23 Tr. Nodding Bells. Sunny, cool. Oriole singing in oaks.	22 42°, 29.85 S, clear, becoming ptly→mostly cldy, gusty	22 29.6R, 45°, clear, →ptly cldy, gusty, NW. Saw single duck every day
24 Tr. Larx. Sunny, cool. Black b. at fountain		23 Same
25 40° at dawn, NW breeze. Splendid Mag. Warbler around fountain	23 45°, 30.0↑ clear, same as 22	24 Same, less wind
	24 41°, 30.25 S, high thin O'cast, then ptly cldy, mild	25 Same, calm. Trapped duck
26 40° again. Dry		26 Same
27 } Same. Mulching, 28 } Watering.	25 52°, 30.1↓, o'cast, lt drizzle, rain 0.4"	
28 Prunus planted		
30. RAIN! 45°, rains, WONDERFUL! 0.26" by noon.	26 52°, 29.85, broken clouds, warm	
31 Another 0.16" by dawn. Clear, lovely	27 42°, 30.4↑, clear, warm, 60s	
Mary Belle, Nuccio, Pavie's Pink, Calsap America	28 40°, 30.5↑, clear warm, 70s	31 3 lines of heavy T-Storms, wind, tornado watch from 6:00 PM to 2:00 AM on 6/1
Blackburnian, Blackpoll Pr. gr. Crested Flycatcher	29 48°, 30.6↑, clear, calm. Warblers, Swainsons Th. + maybe Oriole gone.	
	30 50°, 30.6 S, high thin O'cast,	
3.32"	31 55°, 30.4 ↓, high thin becoming hot	
	Kingbird	

Buttany, Rochelle,
Wiseman, As. Narcissi-
flora, Leni's Aurora,
Mary Belle

Blackburnian, Cape May, much Oriole activity. Maybe Tree Swallows in box- investigating.
Actively at nest- bldg material. 2 Titmice, 4 Titmice Song Chipping, Catbird, Card, Flicker, Wrens, Chicks, Gold + House Finch

1 woodchuck 5/25

JUNE

It was not in the winter

Our loving lot was cast!

It was the time of roses

We plucked them as we passed.

THOMAS HOOD
IT WAS NOT IN THE WINTER

A Summer Herbaceous Border
Lilian Stannard

JUNE

WEEK 1

WEATHER _____

OUTSIDE

VEGETABLES _____

FRUIT _____

FLOWERS _____

BULBS _____

SHRUBS/TREES _____

LAWNS _____

GREENHOUSE _____

NOTES _____

YEAR ......1994......

1 Finished planting
Cambridge haul.

↑

Warm
+
Dry

↓

YEAR ......1995......

Check all pines for caterpillars

1 } 1+07 - 90-18h
2 } + dry

3 Muggy.
R. Calsap,
Caterpillers on Bergin
Pines killed by
Orphane.
R. Casanova
JUMPING SQUIRRELS!

4 0.3" overnight
R. Nuance beginning.

5 } Clear, warm, dry.
6 } Installed drip
lines, mulching.
Lots of young finch,
starling,
grackles.

Inseparable pair
of catbirds about.
Late nesters?

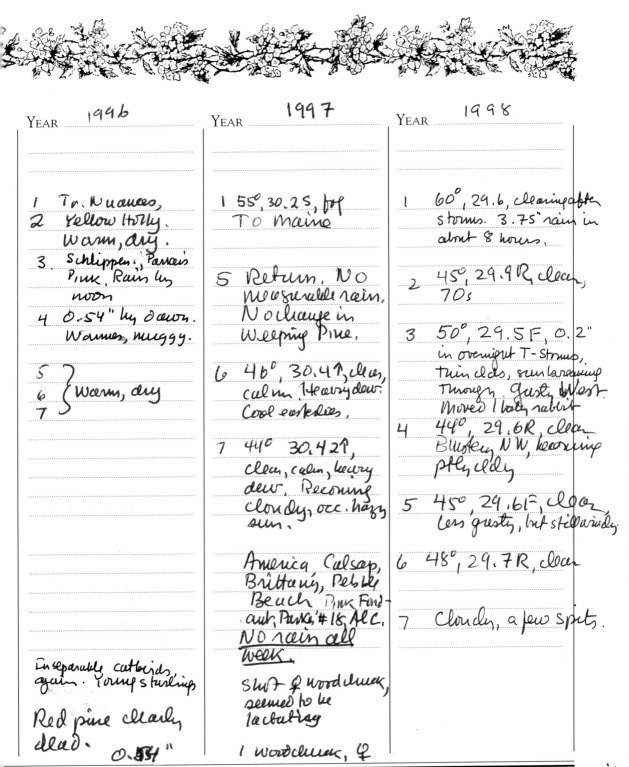

YEAR 1996	YEAR 1997	YEAR 1998

1996

1 Tr. Nuances,
2 Yellow Holly.
Warm, dry.

3 Schlippen·, Parvais
Pink, Rain by
noon

4 0.54" by dawn.
Warmer, muggy.

5 ⎫
6 ⎬ Warm, dry
7 ⎭

Inseparable catbirds,
again. Young starlings

Red pine clearly
dead. 0.54"

1997

1 55°, 30.25, fog
To Maine

5 Return. No
measurable rain.
No change in
Weeping Pine.

6 46°, 30.4↑, clear,
calm. Heavy dew.
Cool easterlies.

7 44° 30.42↑,
clear, calm, heavy
dew. Becoming
cloudy, occ. hazy
sun.

America, Calsap,
Brittany, Pebble
Beach, Pink Ford-
aut. Parke·#18 ALC.
No rain all
week.

Shot ♀ woodchuck,
seemed to be
lactating

1 woodchuck, ♀

1998

1 60°, 29.6, clearing after
storms. 3.75" rain in
about 8 hours.

2 45°, 29.9R, clear,
70s

3 50°, 29.5F, 0.2"
in overnight T-storms,
thin clds, sun breaking
through, gusty West.
Moved 1 baby rabbit

4 44°, 29.6R, clear.
Blustery NW, becoming
ptly. cldy.

5 45°, 29.6F, clear,
less gusty, but still windy

6 48°, 29.7R, clear

7 Cloudy, a few spits.

Trapped + moved 1 rabbit
Shot 1 chuck, 6/7

JUNE

WEEK 2

WEATHER _____

OUTSIDE

  VEGETABLES _____

  FRUIT _____

  FLOWERS _____

  BULBS _____

  SHRUBS/TREES _____

  LAWNS _____

GREENHOUSE _____

NOTES _____

YEAR 1994

7   .15" rain

DRY

12   .25" rain
   Dug 2 Junipers
   from front
13   .38" rain

YEAR 1995

7   .24" overnight

8   .66 in gauge
  Humid, then
  sea breeze, then
  showers. Tr.
  Eric. Roseum (?)
  into woods. (R,
  Al Clifford)

9   0.09" in gauge

10 Transplanted
  Trillium, dug
  stumps. Single
  catbird: Are
  sitting on eggs?

  Robin on lawn—
  first time for
  many days.

12 Fert. Lawn
   Drizzles
13 Baby woodchucks!
  showers

Year 1996	Year 1997	Year 1998

1996

8 Warm, muggy, becoming cool

9 Morning thunder + downpours, 0.8" Ay evening

10 Drizzly, some hazy sun. Mulching, burlap, netting.

11 Very humid, sun by 7:00 AM. mulch, etc.

12 Same. Mulch, re-work nursery swales.

14 Hot spell breaks.

Baby woodchucks

1997

8 45°, 30.4↓, clear. Heavy dew, mist on field. Warming to 60s

9. 40°, 30.4 S, clear, heavy dew. 70s.

10 54°, 30.2↓ dew morning clouds → hot, hazy, 90° Woodchuck ♂

11 62°, 30.0↓, clear, no dew. Skunk at pre-dawn. 92°

12 58°, 29.9↓, clear, skunk again — beautiful. Heavy dew. On-shore breeze 60s all day. 93° inland

13 55°, 29.7↓, ocast. Dew. Becoming hot, scattered ww storms.

14 Away

No Rain

1 Woodchuck, ♂

1998

8 50s, ptly sunny. Shot 1 chuck

9 60s, mild, clear, calm. Saw another chuck.

10 54°, 30.3 S, clear. Shot ♀ chuck. Perhaps got another in hole.

11 52°, 30.3 R, clear

12 6" of rain, at which point gauge overflowed

↓

15

2 or 3 baby woodchucks, 1 adult around

>6" rain

 # JUNE

WEEK 3

WEATHER _____

OUTSIDE

  VEGETABLES _____

  FRUIT _____

  FLOWERS _____

  BULBS _____

  SHRUBS/TREES _____

  LAWNS _____

GREENHOUSE _____

NOTES _____

YEAR ___1994___

14 To Maine,
   with 2 Junipers

Dry ✓

21

YEAR ___1995___

14 0.26 in gauge
   To Maine

17 Return.
   0.25 in gauge.
   HOT

18 90's

19 90's

20 Heat moderates

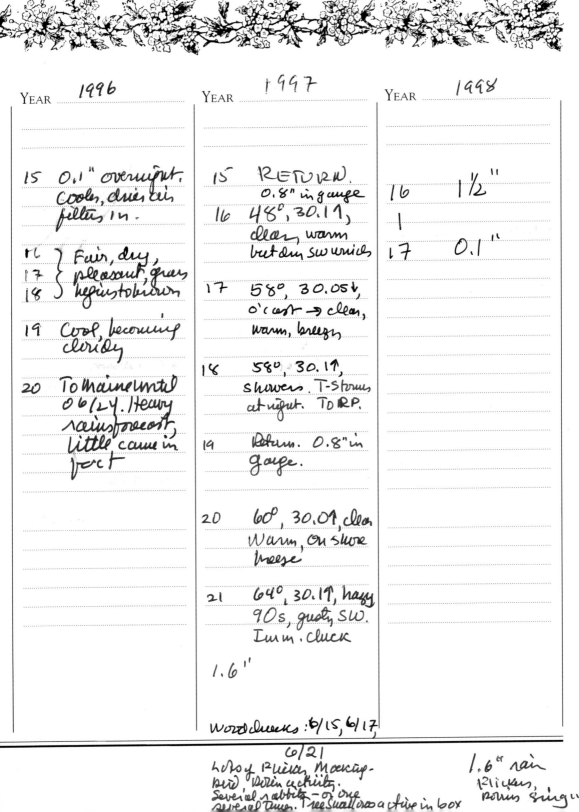

YEAR _1996_

15 0.1" overnight.
    Cooler, drier air
    filters in.

16 ⎫ Fair, dry,
17 ⎬ pleasant, grass
18 ⎭ beginning to brown

19 Cool, becoming
    cloudy

20 To Maine until
    06/24. Heavy
    rains forecast,
    little came in
    fact

YEAR _1997_

15 RETURN.
    0.8" in gauge

16 48°, 30.11,
    clear, warm
    but dry SW winds

17 58°, 30.05↓,
    o'cast → clear,
    warm, breezy

18 58°, 30.1↑,
    showers. T-storms
    at night. TO R.P.

19 Return. 0.8" in
    gauge.

20 60°, 30.09, clear
    warm, on shore
    breeze

21 64°, 30.1↑, hazy
    90s, gusty SW.
    Imm. chuck

1.6"

Woodchucks: 6/15, 6/17,
6/21
Lots of bird, Mocking-
bird, Robin activity.
Several rabbits - or one
several times. Tree Swallows active in box

YEAR _1998_

16   1½"

1

17   0.1"

1.6" rain
flickers,
Robins singing

JUNE

WEEK 4

WEATHER _____

OUTSIDE

YEAR _____1994_____   YEAR _____1995_____

VEGETABLES _____

22   21 Heat breaks,
                                but still dry

FRUIT _____

                            24 Still dry.
                                Baby downy
                                w/ Mama @
                                suet feeder

FLOWERS _____

26 Return for   New mosquito hat
    a few days.   Turns muggy
    Very dry.
    Watering system

BULBS _____

    seems to work.   25 Muggy, hot

SHRUBS/TREES _____

                                No rain

LAWNS _____

                            28 To Maine

GREENHOUSE _____

NOTES _____

            0.78" rain   1.78" rain

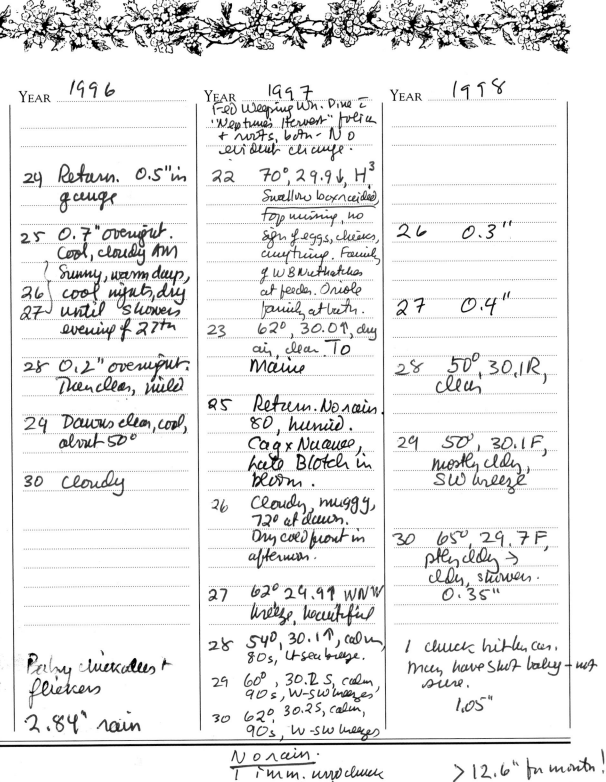

YEAR 1996	YEAR 1997	YEAR 1998

YEAR 1996

29 Return. 0.5" in gauge

25 0.7" overnight. Cool, cloudy AM

26 } Sunny, warm days, cool nights, dry
27 } until showers evening of 27th

28 0.2" overnight. Then clear, mild

29 Dawns clear, cool, about 50°

30 Cloudy

Baby chickadees + flickers

2.84" rain

YEAR 1997

Fed Weeping Wh. Pine — "Neptune's Harvest" foliar + roots, both - No evident change.

22 70°, 29.9↓, H³
Swallow box re-added, top missing, no sign of eggs, chicks, anything. Family of W.B. Nuthatches at feeder. Oriole family at bath.

23 62°, 30.0↑, dry air, clear. TO Maine

25 Return. No rain. 80, humid. Cog x Nucaue, Late Blotch in bloom.

26 Cloudy, muggy, 72° at dawn. Dry cold front in afternoon.

27 62° 24.9↑ WNW breeze, beautiful

28 54°, 30.1↑, calm, 80s, Lt sea breeze.

29 60°, 30.2 ↓ S, calm, 90s, W-SW breezes.

30 62°, 30.25, calm, 90s, W-SW breezes

YEAR 1998

26 0.3"

27 0.4"

28 50°, 30.1R, clear

29 50°, 30.1F, mostly cldy, SW breeze

30 65°, 29.7 F, ptly cldy → cldy, showers. 0.35"

1 chuck hit her car. May have shot baby — not sure.
1.05"

No rain.
1 imm. wood chuck
Month: 1.6" rain
6 wood chucks - Sbu you

> 12.6" for month!

JULY

The kiss of the sun for pardon,
The song of the birds for mirth,
One is nearer God's Heart in a garden,
Than anywhere else on earth.

DOROTHY FRANCES GURNEY
GOD'S GARDEN

The Lily Border at Tagley Manor
Thomas H. Hunn

JULY

WEEK 1

WEATHER _____

OUTSIDE

   VEGETABLES _____

   FRUIT _____

   FLOWERS _____

   BULBS _____

   SHRUBS/TREES _____

   LAWNS _____

GREENHOUSE _____

NOTES _____

YEAR 1994

Drought!

YEAR 1995

3 Return from RP
No rain in quar.
No - or very few
mosquitos.
Start watering +
weeding.

4 Titmouse family -
4 young ones -
at suet.

5 Young chickadees.

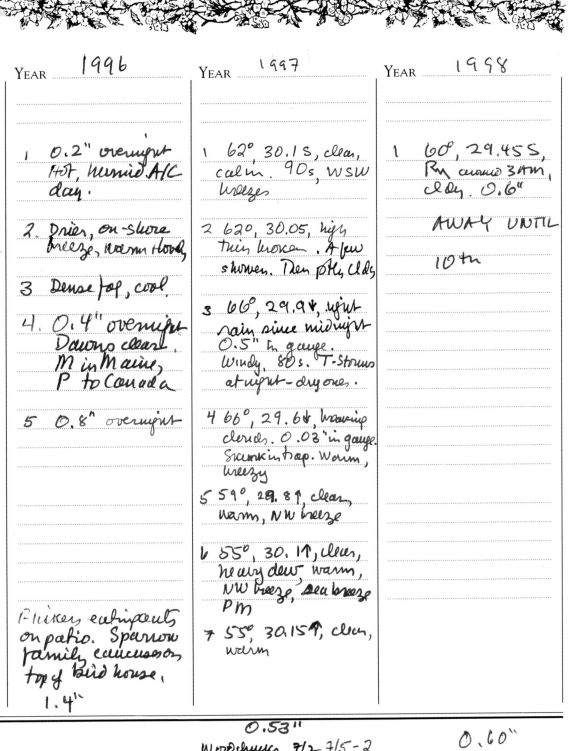

YEAR 1996

1. 0.2" overnight. Hot, humid. A/C day.

2. Drier, on-shore breeze, warm, cloudy.

3. Dense fog, cool.

4. 0.4" overnight. Dawns clear. M in Maine, P to Canada

5. 0.8" overnight

Flickers eating ants on patio. Sparrow family caucuses on top of bird house.

1.4"

YEAR 1997

1. 62°, 30.15, clear, calm. 90s, WSW breezes

2. 62°, 30.05, high thin broken. A few showers. Then ptly cldy

3. 66°, 29.9↓, light rain since midnight. 0.5" in gauge. Windy. 80s. T-storms at night — dry ones.

4. 66°, 29.6↓, heaving clouds. 0.03" in gauge. Skunk in trap. Warm, breezy

5. 59°, 29.8↑, clear, warm, NW breeze

6. 55°, 30.1↑, clear, heavy dew, warm, NW breeze, sea breeze PM

7. 55°, 30.15↑, clear, warm

0.53"

Woodchucks 7/2 7/5 - 2 for week, 10 for year
Robins singing again. 12 Flickers

YEAR 1998

1. 60°, 29.45 S, Rn around 3AM, cldy. 0.6"

AWAY UNTIL

10th

0.60"

JULY

WEEK 2

WEATHER _____

OUTSIDE

  VEGETABLES _____

  FRUIT _____

  FLOWERS _____

  BULBS _____

  SHRUBS/TREES _____

  LAWNS _____

GREENHOUSE _____

NOTES _____

YEAR _1994_

Drought + very hot

10 Deep watered all trees

YEAR _1995_

In Maine all week.

Dry, hot spell cot end of week. Thunderstorm, about 0.10" only.

0.10"

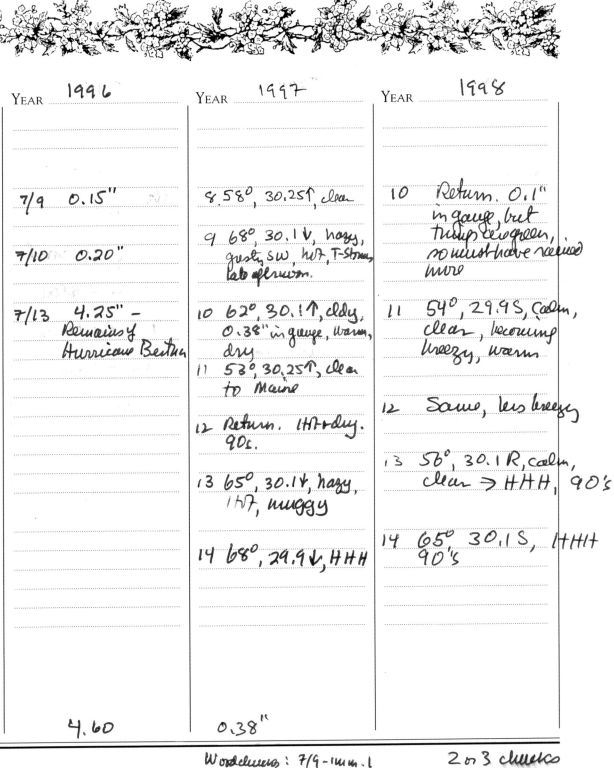

YEAR 1996	YEAR 1997	YEAR 1998
7/9 0.15"	8. 58°, 30.25↑, clear	10 Return. 0.1" in gauge, but tulips evergreen, so must have rained more
7/10 0.20"	9 68°, 30.1↓, hazy, gusty SW, hot, T-Storm, late afternoon.	
7/13 4.25" – Remains of Hurricane Bertha	10 62°, 30.1↑, cldy, 0.38" in gauge, warm, dry	11 54°, 29.95, calm, clear, becoming breezy, warm
	11 53°, 30.25↑, clear to Maine	
	12 Return. Ht+dry. 90s.	12 Same, less breezy
	13 65°, 30.1↓, hazy, hot, muggy	13 58°, 30.1 R, calm, clear → HHH, 90's
	14 68°, 29.9↓, HHH	14 65° 30.1 S, HHH 90's
4.60	0.38"	

Woodchucks: 7/9 – 1mm. 1

2 or 3 chucks
0.10"

 # JULY

WEEK 3

WEATHER _____

OUTSIDE

   VEGETABLES _____

   FRUIT _____

   FLOWERS _____

   BULBS _____

   SHRUBS/TREES _____

   LAWNS _____

GREENHOUSE _____

NOTES _____

YEAR _1994_

Drought ...
very hot

YEAR _1995_

16 Hot spell broken, but still dry. Started watering everything.

17 RAIN!!

18 0.70" in gauge at 7:30 AM

0.70"

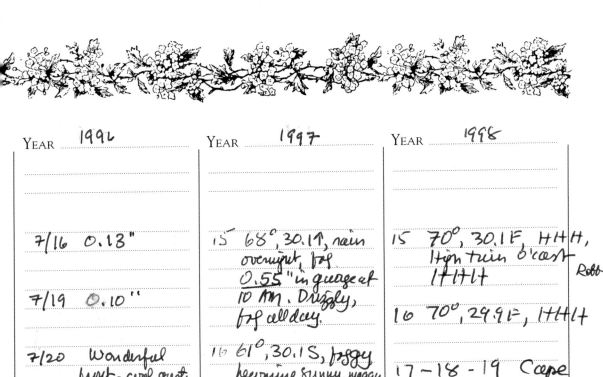

YEAR 1992	YEAR 1997	YEAR 1998

1992

7/16 0.13"

7/19 0.10"

7/20 Wonderful
front- cool, gusty,
dry.

7/21 Same

Lots of young birds.
Robins singing again.
But where are the
catbirds?

0.23"

1997

15 68°, 30.1↑, rain
overnight, fog.
0.55" in gauge at
10 AM. Drizzly,
fog all day.

16 61°, 30.1S, foggy
becoming sunny, muggy

17 65°, 30.0↓, clear
1↑HH, 95°, dry
Th.St.

18 68°, 29.8↓, clear,
HHH, 90s, then
dry cold front

19 64°, 29.75↑, clear,
dry, cool NW est
winds, nice fall.

20 53°, 30.1↑, clear,
warm, NW-W breezy

21 58°, 30.1↓, cldy,
occ. drizzle

tot. 0.55"

1998

15 70°, 30.1F, HHH,
lt'gn rain o'cast
1↑1↑1↑   Rabbit

16 70°, 29.9F, 1↑H1↑

17-18-19 Cape
Basically 1↑o↑- len
humid

20 65°, 30.1F, HHH
Evening ☈

21 64, 30.0R, Clear
0.5" 85-ish,
breezy; not too humid

22 68, 29.95, clear
1↑H'1↑ - 92°

0.5"
2 chucks

JULY

WEEK 4

WEATHER _____

OUTSIDE

VEGETABLES _____

FRUIT _____

FLOWERS _____

BULBS _____

SHRUBS/TREES _____

LAWNS _____

GREENHOUSE _____

NOTES _____

YEAR 1994

24 - Deep-watered
all trees.
2 red pines have
lost leaders

Drought +
few ...

Nursery bed in
woods doing
well, as is
vinca on bank.

Sprayed for
bittersweet — also
cut — +
poison ivy.

- O -

YEAR 1995

26 H-H-H.
0.5" in rain
gauge on arrival

T-Storms, another
0.95" in
evening

27 Sprayed poison
ivy, lawn
weeds,
H-H-H again.

One new Rhodo-
dendron — 1 of 2
dead.

1.45"

7.68"/month

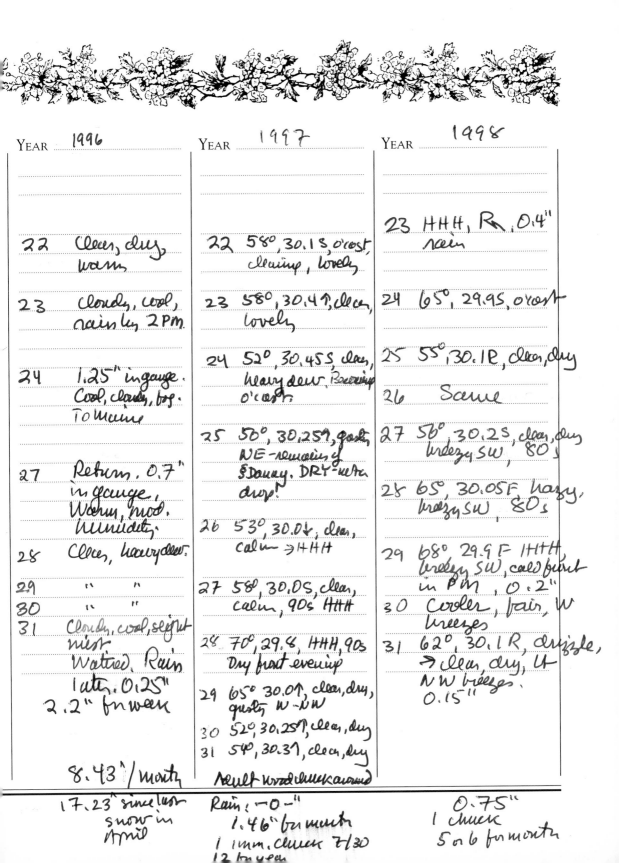

YEAR 1996	YEAR 1997	YEAR 1998
		23 HHH, R↘, 0.4" rain
22 Clear, dry, warm	22 58°, 30.18 o'cast, clearing, lovely	
23 Cloudy, cool, rain by 2 PM.	23 58°, 30.41↑, clear, lovely	24 65°, 29.95, o'cast
24 1.25" in gauge. Cool, cloudy, fog. To Maine.	24 52°, 30.45S, clear, heavy dew. Becoming o'cast.	25 55°, 30.1R, clear, dry
		26 Same
	25 50°, 30.25↑, gusty NE—remains of §Danny. DRY—not a drop!	27 56°, 30.2S, clear, dry breezy SW, 80's
27 Return, 0.7" in gauge. Warm, mod. humidity.	26 53°, 30.0↑, clear, calm →HHH	28 65°, 30.05F, hazy, breezy SW, 80s
28 Clear, heavy dew.	27 58°, 30.0S, clear, calm, 90s HHH	29 68°, 29.9 F HHH, breezy SW, dew point in PM, 0.2"
29 " "	28 70°, 29.8, HHH, 90s Dry front evening	30 Cooler, fair, W breezes
30 " "	29 65° 30.0↑, clear, dry, gusty W-NW	31 62°, 30.1R, drizzle, → clear, dry, lt NW breezes. 0.15"
31 Cloudy, cool, slight mist. Watered. Rain late. 0.25". 2.2" for week	30 52°, 30.25↑, clear, dry	
	31 54°, 30.3↑, clear, dry	
8.43"/ month	Adult woodchuck around	

17.23" since last snow in April

Rain: −0−"
1.46" for month
1 imm. chuck 7/30
12 for year

0.75"
1 chuck
5 or 6 for month

AUGUST

I know a little garden close
Thick with lily and red rose,

Where I would wander if I might

From dewy dawn to dewy night,

And have one with me wandering.

WILLIAM MORRIS
THE LIFE AND DEATH OF JASON

View of a Country House and Garden
Ernest Arthur Rowe

AUGUST

WEEK 1

WEATHER _____

OUTSIDE

   VEGETABLES _____

   FRUIT _____

   FLOWERS _____

   BULBS _____

   SHRUBS/TREES _____

   LAWNS _____

GREENHOUSE _____

NOTES _____

YEAR __1994__

7 Drought broken.
Weeded south
edge, among
rhododendrons (some
still in bloom),
and north lawn.
Attacked bittersweet
and poison ivy.

Mosquitos

YEAR __1995__

3 A good rain.

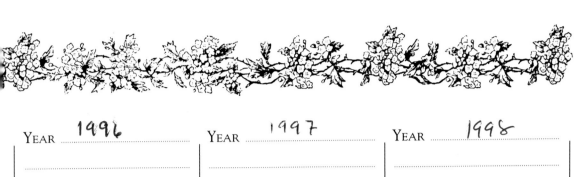

Year 1996	Year 1997	Year 1998

1996

1 Cool, drizzly

3 Hazy, Hot Humid
4 " " "
5 " " "
6 " " "
7 " " "

Watered everything
on 6, 7 + 8. No
rain since 7/31.

1997

1 56°, 30.3↓, clear
H+H-90s

2 66°, 30.1↓, hazy,
HHH-90s

3 65, 29.95, heavy dew
Front passes, m, hail
0.70" in gauge
1 chuck

4 65°, 30.09, o'cast,
cool moist NE. 1 chuck
Sowed grass

5 58°, 30.0↓ o'cast.
lt rain overnight:
0.10" only. Sowed
grass.

6 30.1↑, ptly cldy,
warm

7 30.25↑, 54°,
clear, dew

1998

1 58°, 30.2R, clear,
I 80

2 54°, 30.4S, clear

Fair, warm,
dry

7 0.3" Rain

0.80"
1 chuck 8/3 ⎱ 14 for
" 8/4 ⎰ year
Bad mosquito week

0.30"

 # AUGUST

WEEK 2

WEATHER _____

OUTSIDE

  VEGETABLES _____

  FRUIT _____

  FLOWERS _____

  BULBS _____

  SHRUBS/TREES _____

  LAWNS _____

GREENHOUSE _____

NOTES _____

YEAR *1994*

15 0.8" in
gauge.
Lawns look
OK.

Met with Jay
T. re fence
level problem.
Bad mosquitos

YEAR *1995*

10 Return from
Maine.
grass pretty good,
bubbler full.

1.5" in gauge

Mosquitos bad
first day, then
O.K. for next
two.

Year 1996	Year 1997	Year 1998

8 First tomato
picked - not quite
fully ripe yet.
H-H-H still.
To Maine for a
week.

Tomatos!
Grass sprouts

8 HHH

9 60°, 30.5 R,
clear, HHH

10 65°, 30.25 F,
HHH

11 70°, 29.9 F
Broad clds, HH

13   1.25"

12. 65°, 30.0 R, Thunderstorms
overnight + in AM. 0.1"

13 55°, 30.3 R, clear,
lovely 1.25" yesterday

14 Same

1.25" for week   1.35"

 # AUGUST

WEEK 3

WEATHER _____

OUTSIDE

   VEGETABLES _____

   FRUIT _____

   FLOWERS _____

   BULBS _____

   SHRUBS/TREES _____

   LAWNS _____

GREENHOUSE _____

NOTES _____

YEAR _1994_

YEAR _1995_

17 Back from Me.
18 Warm, dry,
19 cool nights —
   we arrived at a
   cool front.

Many young
robins, finches,
also cardinals
+ downy wood-
peckers titmice,
nuthatch, chicka-
dees. And wood
chucks. And
mosquitos.

20 50° at 0 day!
Mosquitos!

YEAR 1996	YEAR 1997	YEAR 1998
16 Return from ME. 2" in rain gauge. Clear, warm, dry days, cool nights.	17 0.28"	15 Breezy SW, warm
		16 60°, 30.1R, warm
		17 65° rain + drizzle 0.5"
		18 65°, 30.0 F, foggy, HHH, 80, Rain, 0.25"
21 Started watering	21 1.75"	19 55°, 30.2R, rain o'cast, NW dry breeze
	22 0.38"	
		20 50°, 30.4R, crystal clear gorgeous
		21 Same
23 Return to ME.		
		22 55°, 30.2F, same
	2.41"	0.75"

AUGUST

WEEK 4

WEATHER _____

OUTSIDE

VEGETABLES _____

FRUIT _____

FLOWERS _____

BULBS _____

SHRUBS/TREES _____

LAWNS _____

GREENHOUSE _____

NOTES _____

YEAR 1994

YEAR 1995

28 0.2" in gauge.
2 demon Drops
look very dew.
Mosquitos!

29 45° at dawn!

TO R.P.

until 9/6

30   3.25" in gauge.
All OK. except
– Rt. Hand Red Pine –
nearest Begins –
Some sort of enclosed
borer. Also
in 2 pines along
Walsh fence
Mosquitos

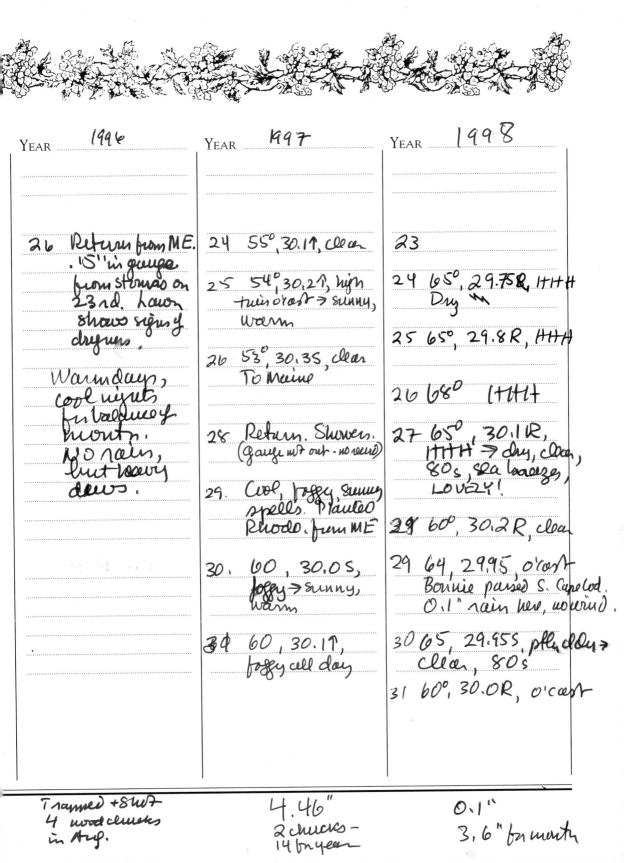

YEAR _1996_

26 Return from ME.
."S" in gauge
from storms on
23rd. Lawn
shows signs of
dryness.

Warm days,
cool nights
for balance of
month.
No rain,
but heavy
dews.

YEAR _1997_

24 55°, 30.1↑, clear

25 54°, 30.2↑, high
    thin o'cast → sunny,
    warm

26 53°, 30.35, clear
    To Maine

28 Return. Showers.
    (gauge not out - no read)

29. Cool, foggy, sunny
     spells. Planted
     Rhodo. from ME

30. 60, 30.0S,
     foggy → sunny,
     warm

30 60, 30.1↑,
    foggy all day

YEAR _1998_

23

24 65°, 29.75R, HHH
    Dry ⚡

25 65°, 29.8R, HHH

26 68° HHH

27 65°, 30.1R,
    HHH' → dry, clear,
    80s, sea breeze,
    LOVELY!

28 60°, 30.2R, clear

29 64, 29.95, o'cast
    Bonnie passed S. Cape Cod.
    0.1" rain here, no wind.

30 65, 29.95S, p'tly cldy →
    clear, 80s

31 60°, 30.0R, o'cast

T rained +shot
4 woodchucks
in Aug.

4.46"
2 chucks -
14 for year

0.1"
3.6" for month

SEPTEMBER

Sure, I said, heav'n did not mean,
Where I reap thou shouldst but glean,
Lay thy sheaf adown and come,
Share my harvest and my home.

THOMAS HOOD
RUTH

Late September
Lilian Stannard

SEPTEMBER

WEEK 1

WEATHER _____

OUTSIDE
  VEGETABLES _____

FRUIT _____

FLOWERS _____

BULBS _____

SHRUBS/TREES _____

LAWNS _____

GREENHOUSE _____

NOTES _____

YEAR __1994__

1 Cold front - cool, clear, lovely.

3 42° at 7 AM
Flicker, Y B
Sapsucker, hordes
of P. Finch

Probably not sapsucker, but immature downy

YEAR __1995__

One white pine
at top ridge by
Norris's dead.

6 Returned.
Very dry.

Started converting
lawn around
spruce tree into
bed.

No rain, not
much dew
Robins, Flickers

At Plum Is. Snow
Egrets, Semipal. Plover,
Dunlin,

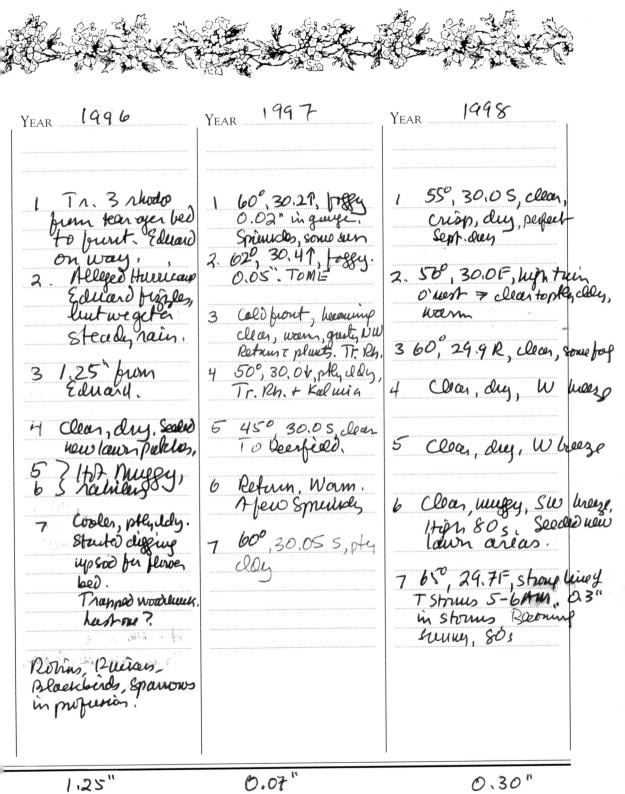

YEAR 1996	YEAR 1997	YEAR 1998
1 Tr. 3 rhodo from rear gar bed to front. Eduard on way.	1 60°, 30.2↑, foggy 0.02" in gauge. Sprinkles, some sun	1 55°, 30.0 S, clear, crisp, dry, perfect Sept. day
2. Alleged Hurricane Eduard fizzles, but we get a steady rain.	2. 62°, 30.4↑, foggy. 0.05". TOM↑	2. 58°, 30.0 F, high thin o'cast ⇒ clear to ptly cldy, warm
3 1.25" from Eduard.	3 Cold front, becoming clear, warm, gusty NW Return plants. Tr. Rh.	3 60°, 29.9 R, clear, some fog
4 Clear, dry. Seeded new lawn patches.	4 50°, 30.0↑, ptly cldy, Tr. Rh. + Kalmia	4 Clear, dry, W breeze
5 ⎱ Hot, muggy,	5 45°, 30.0 S, clear ↑ ○ Deerfield.	5 Clear, dry, W breeze
6 ⎰ rainless	6 Return. Warm. A few Sprinkles	6 Clear, muggy, SW breeze, high 80s. Seeded new lawn areas.
7 Cooler, ptly cldy. Started digging up sod for flower bed. Trapped woodchuck. Last one ?	7 60°, 30.05 S, ptly cldy	7 65°, 29.7 F, strong line of T Storms 5–6 AM. 0.3" in storms. Becoming sunny, 80s
Robins, Buntings, Blackbirds, Sparrows in profusion.		

1.25"	0.07"	0.30"

Seeded new lawn areas

SEPTEMBER

WEEK 2

WEATHER _____

OUTSIDE

  VEGETABLES _____

  FRUIT _____

  FLOWERS _____

  BULBS _____

  SHRUBS/TREES _____

  LAWNS _____

GREENHOUSE _____

NOTES _____

YEAR ___1994___

YEAR ___1995___

8   Continued very
    dry

13

Robins, Flickers

At Plum Is.
Snowies, Semipals,
Dunlin, Golden
Plover

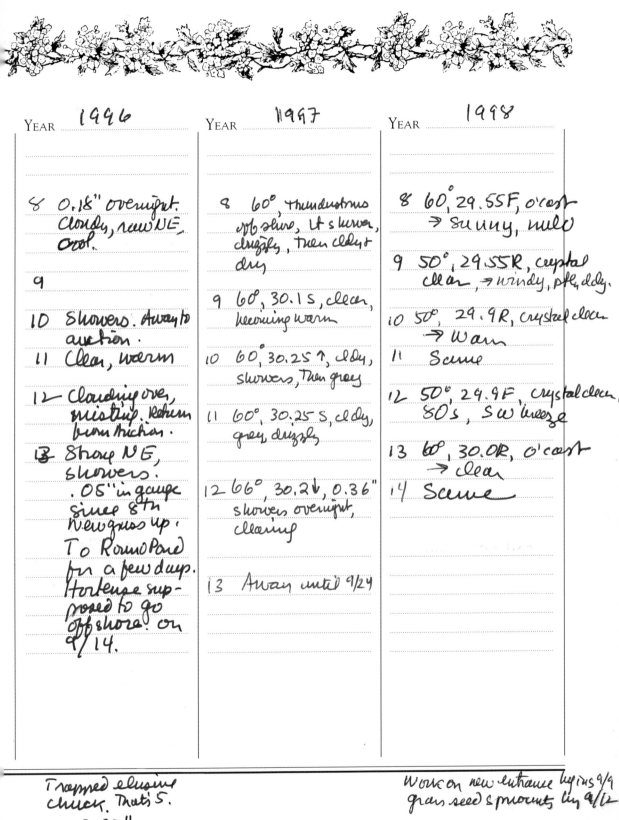

Year 1996	Year 1997	Year 1998
8 0.18" overnight. Cloudy, raw NE, cool.	8 60° thunderstorms off shore, lt shower, drizzly, then cldy + dry	8 60°, 29.55F, o'cast → sunny, mild
9	9 60°, 30.15, clear, becoming warm	9 50°, 29.55R, crystal clear → windy, ptly cldy.
10 Showers. Away to auction.	10 60°, 30.25↑, cldy, showers, then grey	10 50°, 29.9R, crystal clear → warm
11 Clear, warm	11 60°, 30.25 S, cldy, grey, drizzly	11 Same
12 Clouding over, misting. Return from auction.	12 66°, 30.2↓, 0.36" showers overnight, clearing	12 50°, 29.9F, crystal clear 80's, SW breeze
13 Sharp NE, showers. .05" in gauge since 8th. New grass up. To Round Pond for a few days. Hortense supposed to go offshore on 9/14.	13 Away until 9/24	13 60°, 30.0R, o'cast → clear
		14 Same

Trapped elusive chuck. That's 5. 0-23"

Work on new entrance begins 9/9. grass seed sprouts by 9/12.

SEPTEMBER

WEEK 3

WEATHER _____

OUTSIDE
   VEGETABLES _____

   FRUIT _____

   FLOWERS _____

   BULBS _____

   SHRUBS/TREES _____

   LAWNS _____

GREENHOUSE _____

NOTES _____

YEAR 1994

15 1.2" in rain
gauge. Lawn
in fine shape.

Screech Owl
whinnies around
4:00 AM.

Fewer mosquitos

17 Hot, humid, PM
T-Storms

18 0.8" Rain since
preceding PM

Golden Plover, gr. Yellowlegs
on Flats

Put Ringer Winterstra
on lawn.

YEAR 1995

15 0.1" in
rain gauge.

17 2.0", at
last.
But just a
drop in the
bucket.

20 Start watering
again, esp;
trees!

2 truck-loads
of manure from
Susan Olbrych.

Finished digging
peat around
spruce.

21 To Muineto
long weekend

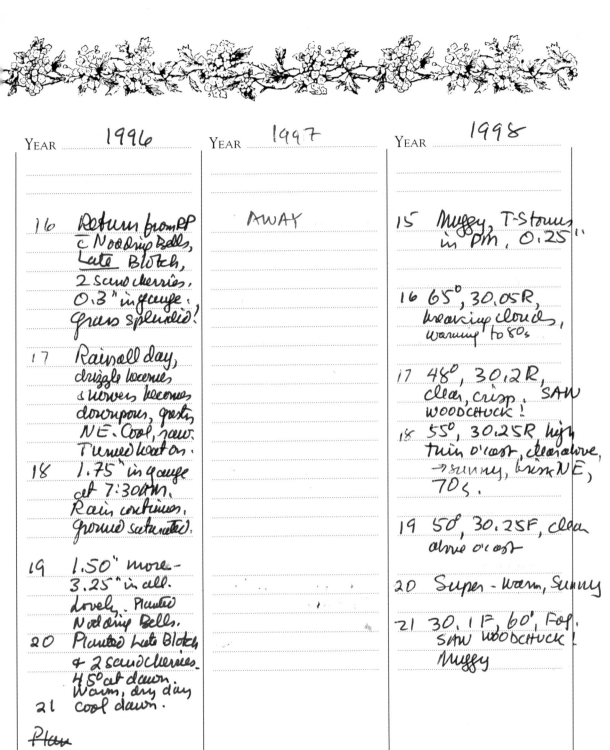

YEAR 1996	YEAR 1997	YEAR 1998

1996

16 Return from RP c̄ Nodding Bells, Late Blotch, 2 sand cherries. 0.3" in gauge! Grass splendid!

17 Rain all day, drizzle becomes showers becomes downpour, gusty NE. Cool, raw. Turned heat on.

18 1.75" in gauge at 7:30 AM. Rain continues, ground saturated.

19 1.50" more — 3.25" in all. lovely. Planted Nodding Bells.

20 Planted Late Blotch & 2 sand cherries. 45° at dawn. Warm, dry day

21 cool dawn.

Plan

1997

AWAY

1998

15 Muggy, T-Storms in PM. 0.25"

16 65°, 30.05R, breaking clouds, warming to 80s

17 48°, 30.2R, clear, crisp. SAW WOODCHUCK!

18 55°, 30.25R high thin o'cast, clear above, → sunny, brisk NE, 70s.

19 50°, 30.25F, clear above o'cast

20 Super - warm, sunny

21 30.1F, 60°, Fog. SAW WOODCHUCK! Muggy

Heat on for first time. Shot another woodchuck. 6 in all. 3.55" in week

denis Aurora blooming! Shot 1 woodchuck Saw another 0.25"

September

Week 4

Weather _____

Outside

    Vegetables _____

    Fruit _____

    Flowers _____

    Bulbs _____

    Shrubs/Trees _____

    Lawns _____

Greenhouse _____

Notes _____

Year __1994__

23   3.5" rain.

Year __1995__

22 } Rain
23 }

24 Return.
0.5" in
gauge.

Lawn coming
back a bit.

26 0.5" of
rain
drizzle

27 To New
Mexico for
2 weeks

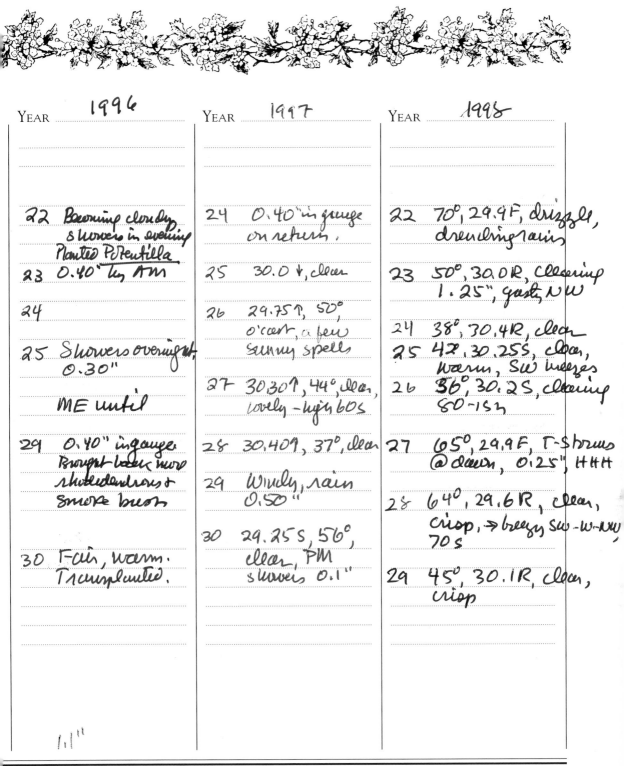

Year	1996	Year	1997	Year	1998

1996

22 Becoming cloudy, showers in evening. Planted Potentilla

23 0.40" by AM

24

25 Showers overnight, 0.30"

ME until

29 0.40" in gauge. Brought back more rhododendrons & smoke bush

30 Fair, warm. Transplanted.

1.1"

6.13" in month

1997

24 0.40" in gauge on return.

25 30.0 ↓, clear

26 29.75 ↑, 50°, o'cast, a few sunny spells

27 30.30 ↑, 44°, clear, lovely - high 60s

28 30.40 ↑, 37°, clear

29 Windy, rain 0.50"

30 29.25 S, 56°, clear, PM showers 0.1"

1.00"
ca. 1.10 for month

1998

22 70°, 29.9 F, drizzle, drenching rains

23 50°, 30.0 R, clearing 1.25", gusty NW

24 38°, 30.4 R, clear

25 42°, 30.25 S, clear, warm, SW breezes

26 36°, 30.2 S, clearing 80-15z

27 65°, 29.9 F, T-storms @ dawn, 0.25", HHH

28 64°, 29.6 R, clear, crisp, → breezy SW-W-NW 70s

29 45°, 30.1 R, clear, crisp

OCTOBER

Season of mists and mellow fruitfulness,

Close bosom-friend of the maturing sun;

Conspiring with him how to load and bless

With fruit the vines that round the thatch

eaves run.

JOHN KEATS
TO AUTUMN

Abberton Church from Rous Lench Court
Ernest Arthur Rowe

OCTOBER

WEEK 1

WEATHER _____

OUTSIDE

    VEGETABLES _____

    FRUIT _____

    FLOWERS _____

    BULBS _____

    SHRUBS/TREES _____

    LAWNS _____

GREENHOUSE _____

NOTES _____

YEAR 1993

6 Started moving
Rhododendrons
to Newbury

9 More moving but
RKH filled nursery
pots.

YEAR 1995

Dug out strip
by fence on
south side,
dug in peat
moss and
compost

1995
In New Mexico

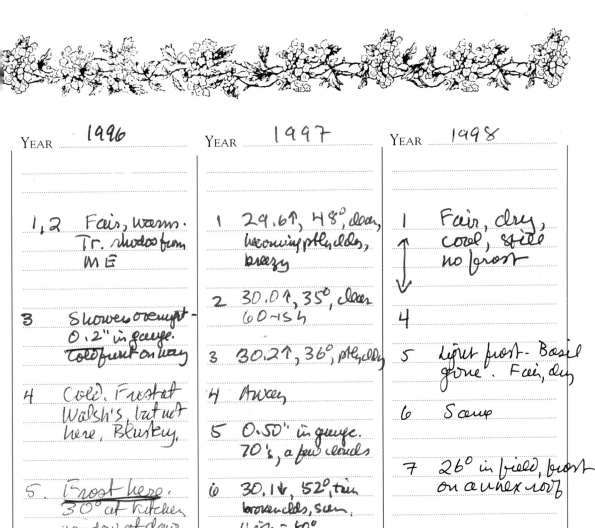

YEAR 1996

1, 2   Fair, warm.
       Tr. shades from
       ME

3   Showers overnight -
       0.2" in gauge.
       Cold front on way

4   Cold. Frost at
       Walsh's, but not
       here. Blustery.

5.   Frost here.
       30° at kitchen
       window at dawn.

6   Frost again. Planted
       bulbs in front, pulled
       tomatoes, basil + the
       casualties

7   More bulbs

BULBS
   Front of house: Tulips
   Front, side garden: Lilies
   Cornus mas: Scilla siberica
                chionidoxa
   N.Side Bank: Scilla

   Wildflower garden: Allium
      roseum + A. Moly
   Fountain: anemone
       blanda, blue+white: scilla
       yellow crocus + tulip silla

YEAR 1997

1   29.6↑, 48° clear,
       becoming ptly cldy,
       breezy

2   30.0↑, 35°, clear
       60-ish

3   30.2↑, 36°, ptly cldy

4   Away

5   0.50" in gauge.
       70's, a few clouds

6   30.1↓, 52°, rain,
       broken clds, sun.
       High = 80°

7   30.2↑, 50°, rain
       o'cast
       To Round Pond

0.50"

YEAR 1998

1   Fair, dry,
       cool, still
↑   no frost
↓

4

5   Light frost - Basil
       gone. Fair, dry

6   Same

7   26° in field, frost
       on annex roof

OCTOBER

WEEK 2

WEATHER _____

OUTSIDE

  VEGETABLES _____

  FRUIT _____

  FLOWERS _____

  BULBS _____

  SHRUBS/TREES _____

  LAWNS _____

GREENHOUSE _____

NOTES _____

YEAR 1994

10   Started using chipper-shredder. Spread chips on bank

13   First frost on grass, roof

YEAR 1995

I N

NEW MEXICO

Rain back east + warm

Weeping Pine somewhat stressed, White Pine on top of hill — further from road — badly stressed.

13   3" in gauge. Lawn, plants look good. Warm, sunny.

14   Flock of white-throats, with a few song sparrows arrive. Sunny, warm.

YEAR 1996	YEAR 1997	YEAR 1998

<table>
<tr><td></td><td>Long watering of everything.</td><td></td></tr>
</table>

1996

8   More bales. Fall fert. on lawn. Rain in evening, gusty NE winds

9   1.65" by morning. Possum in trap. Released, bent down chuck hole.

10
1   Fair, mild balance of week
13

14   Quick morning shower, 0.10", then clear, high 60s

1997

8   Return. Warm, sunny

9   50°, 30.50↑ thin o'cast, sun PM, warm

10   60°, 30.25↓ [o↑] very warm — 80-ish

11   30.50↑ 45° clear, breezy 70-ish

12   30.50↑, 34° clear, 60s, NW breeze becoming onshore

13   30.50 S, 35°, clear

14   30.45↓, 50°, clear

1998

8   Drizzle, showers, occ. heavy

9   54°, 2.5" in gauge, drizzle

    To Deerfield until 11th. Drizzle, rain during period

12   55°, 2.25" in gauge, overcast

13   55° o'cast, dreary, rain

14   AND AGAIN! 0.8"

1.75"	-0"-	5.6"

OCTOBER

WEEK 3

WEATHER _____

OUTSIDE

   VEGETABLES _____

   FRUIT _____

   FLOWERS _____

   BULBS _____

   SHRUBS/TREES _____

   LAWNS _____

GREENHOUSE _____

NOTES _____

YEAR 1994

16 Frost.
started on
strip along drive.

YEAR 1995

15 0.7" in
gauge aft
windy, stormy
night

16 40° at dawn
To R.P. for
2 days

18 Mild, sunny
19 Rain heavy
watering
20 Raw, fog,
drizzle.
Continue heavy
watering.

21 Sharp-shin
Hawk in
Walsh's maple
after birds at
feeder.
Strong SE winds,
showers
1.25" rain
in all

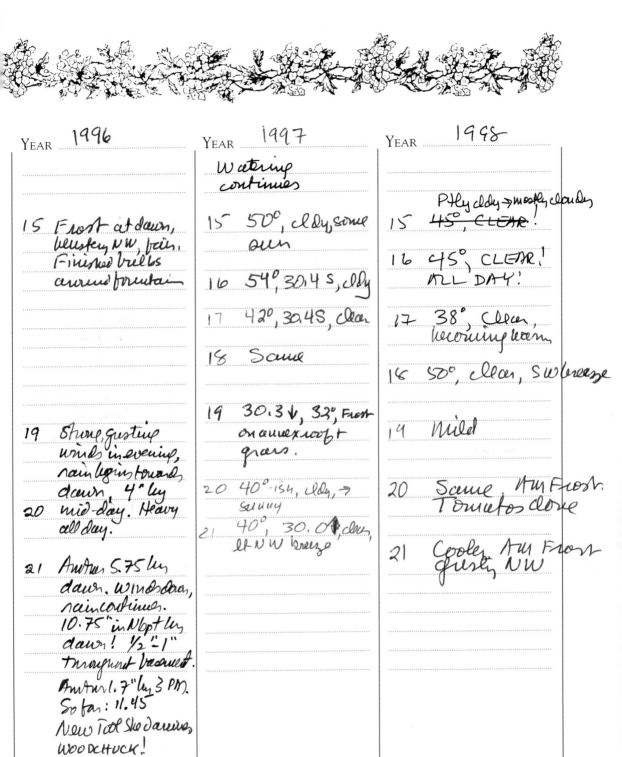

Year 1996	Year 1997	Year 1998
	Watering continues	
15 Frost at dawn, blustery NW, fair, finished trellis around fountain	15 50°, cldy, some sun	15 Ptly cldy → mostly cloudy 45°, CLEAR!
	16 54°, 30.4S, cldy	16 45°, CLEAR! ALL DAY!
	17 42°, 30.4S, clear	17 38°, clear, becoming warm
	18 Same	18 50°, clear, SW breeze
19 Shone, gusting winds in evening, rain begins toward dawn, 4" by	19 30.3↓, 32°, frost on annex roof & grass.	19 Mild
20 mid-day. Heavy all day.	20 40°-ish, cldy → sunny	20 Same, AM frost. Tomatoes done
	21 40°, 30.0, clear, lt NW breeze	21 Cooler, AM Frost gusty NW
21 Another 5.75 by dawn. Winds down, rain continues. 10.75" in Newpt by dawn! ½"-1" throughout Vineyard. Another 1.7" by 3 PM. So far: 11.45 New Tool Shed arrives WOODCHUCK!		
11.45"	-0-"	
Peak color begins towards end of week		

OCTOBER

WEEK 4

WEATHER _____

OUTSIDE
   VEGETABLES _____

FRUIT _____

FLOWERS _____

BULBS _____

SHRUBS/TREES _____

LAWNS _____

GREENHOUSE _____

NOTES _____

YEAR 1994

Drought. No
rain all month
except for 0.25"
mid-month.

Juncos appear
+ leave.

No frost since
10/16.

Took down ash
+ oaks on N.
side.

YEAR 1995

22 Warm. Clean-
up

Warm, heavy
dews, sunny
days

28 SE storm,
strong winds,
1.25" rain

29 Cool, clear,
NW breeze

CLOCK CHANGE

YEAR 1996	YEAR 1997	YEAR 1998
Peak color here this week. Lovely cooks.	Deep Watering continues	
22 13.03" total for storm - official US2T. Cloudy, mild, drizzly.	22 29.9"S, 30°, clear, blustery	22 35°, clear, gusty
		23 35°, clear
23 AM shower, then clearing ⊙ .2" Witch Hazel blooming - mis-labeled "Arnold's Promise"	23 30.1↑, 24°, clear, blustery	24 Warm, sunny
	24 30.2↑, 32°, ptly cldy	25 " "
24 0.05" overnight. Then clear, warm.	25 30.1S, 42°, lt rain ⊙ 0.4" by evening.	26 Cooler, sunny
		27 " "
25 ⎫ mild, 26 ⎪ sunny, 27 ⎬ breezy! 28 ⎪ Color peaks, ⎪ leaves begin 29 ⎭ to drop	26 30.4↑, 30°, clear, becoming cloudy	28 Rain in evening. 0.3"
	28 29.7↓, 44° rain, gusty NE. 0.5"	29 Clearing, gusty NW. 50° at clearin
	28 29.55↑, 36°, ⊙ night showers, 0.05" clear → ptly cldy, gusty NW	↓
30 Cooler, still no frost. 03" in showers.	29 Ptly cldy, gusty NW 7W no frost	Same trend to end of month.
31 Cool, clear. 13.58 -11.45 last week 2.13 this week 15.33" in Oct.	30 34°, 30.25↑, calm, clear, warm, lovely.	
	31 30°, 30.4↑, calm, clear	

Live prop in cellar. Margaret discovers mummifies prop under cellar stairs!

0.95" Rain
4.45" for Month
Drain hoses
Last lawn mowing - No! Also in Nov.

0.30"
5.90 for month

NOVEMBER

Tis down in yonder garden green,
Love, where we used to walk,
The finest flower that ere was seen
Is wither'd on the stalk.

ANON
BALLAD

An Amateur (watercolour)
Frederick Walker

NOVEMBER

WEEK 1

WEATHER _____

OUTSIDE

   VEGETABLES _____

   FRUIT _____

   FLOWERS _____

   BULBS _____

   SHRUBS/TREES _____

   LAWNS _____

GREENHOUSE _____

NOTES _____

YEAR _1994_

1   0.7" rain.

Shredded leaves in chipper.

Dry balance of week.

YEAR _1995_

1   Cold, dank. Shredded.

2   1.25" rain by 4:00 PM.

3 - 6   Mild with a couple of blustery days. Heavy frosts overnight.

7   1.25" rain overnight.

YEAR __1996__

1 Cool, blustery, some sun. Still blooming: Scabious, Shasta Daisy, Penstemon, Coreopsis, And R. Lewis Aurora!

2,3 Cold, blustery

4, 5 mild, still a few flowers, Hauled manure, shredded leaves.

6

7 To Sturbridge for symposium on clocks. Top, drizzle

YEAR __1997__

1 30.4↓, 50°, drizzly 0.05" overnight

2 Rain

3 29.9↑, 46°, clear 2.25" in gauge warm

4 40-ish, clear, warm, evenings cooler

5 30.5↑, 38°, clear, 0.04 in gauge.

6 30.7↑, 32° clear, calm, warm MANURE!

7 30.5↓, 46°, cldy, gusty NE, occ. spits, occ. sunny spells

YEAR __1998__

Still Blooming - same as 1996 pretty much.

1-5 30-ish at dawn, warming to upper 40s - low 50s, partly cloudy, gusty W-NW.

6 25° at dawn. Impatiens finally frosted.

2.25"

 # NOVEMBER

WEEK 2

WEATHER _____

OUTSIDE

VEGETABLES _____

FRUIT _____

FLOWERS _____

BULBS _____

SHRUBS/TREES _____

LAWNS _____

GREENHOUSE _____

NOTES _____

YEAR **1994**

12   Frost, first since 10/16.

More leaves and brush shredding chipping.

Margaret finished planting bulbs.

17-18   Hauled + spread horse manure

18   Rain-light-first since Nov. 1.

YEAR **1995**

8   Clearing, NW winds. To ME

9 } cold snap. 22°
10 } on new thermometer on return from ME.

11   Warm, strong SW winds, rain at night

12   0.60 in gauge. 55° at dawn, 40° by 10 AM, strong gusty NW winds. 34° by 6 PM

13   A few snowflakes, cold all day.

14   NE storm winds up, strong gusty winds, heavy rain by evening. goes on all night.

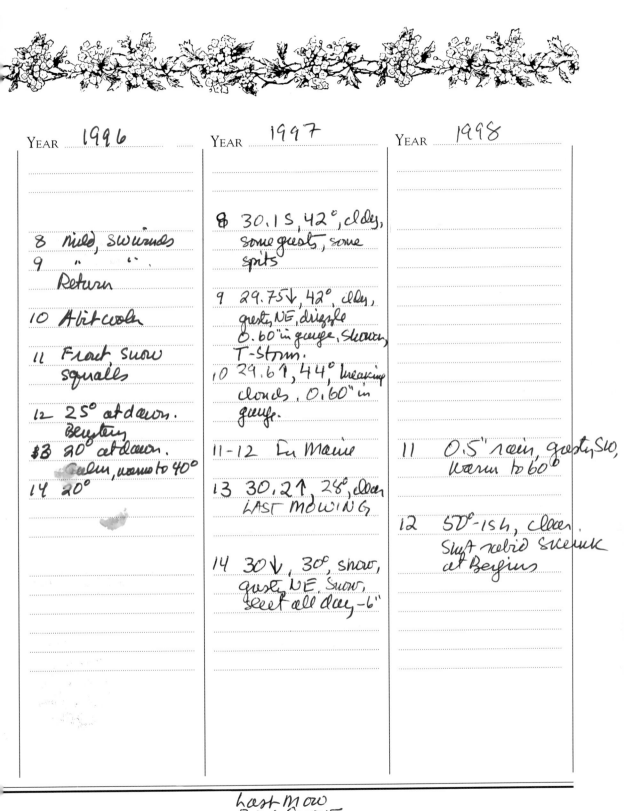

YEAR __1996__

8 Mild, S winds
9 "   "
   Return

10 A bit cooler

11 First snow
    squalls

12 25° at dawn.
    Blustery

13 20° at dawn.
    Calm, warms to 40°

14 20°

YEAR __1997__

8 30.15, 42°, cldy,
   some guests, some
   spits

9 29.75↓, 42°, cldy,
   gusty, NE, drizzle
   0.60" in gauge, showers,
   T-storm.

10 29.6↑, 44°, breaking
    clouds. 0.60" in
    gauge.

11-12 In Maine

13 30.2↑, 28°, clear
    LAST MOWING

14 30↓, 30°, snow,
    gusty NE. Snow,
    sleet all day ~6"

YEAR __1998__

11 0.5" rain, gusty S W,
    warm to 60°

12 50°-15 h, clear.
    Shut rabid skunk
    at Berlins

Last Mow
First Snow

1.20" rain
6.00" snow

 # NOVEMBER

WEEK 3

WEATHER _____

OUTSIDE

   VEGETABLES _____

   FRUIT _____

   FLOWERS _____

   BULBS _____

   SHRUBS/TREES _____

   LAWNS _____

GREENHOUSE _____

NOTES _____

YEAR __1994__

19 1.15" of rain overnight
    Warm

22 0.8" of rain overnight
    Starts to turn cooler. No hard frost yet.

23 SNOW! Just flurries. Under 32° all day 20° by evening

YEAR __1995__

15 3.74" in guage at 9:00AM from NE storm. 45°

20 - 27
  Away for a week.

  Appears to have been some rain.

  (Thelma's Madison, WI, for Thanksgiving)

YEAR 1996	YEAR 1997	YEAR 1998

1996

15 20s again.
16 Moderating
17 Upper 50s

18 36 at dawn

19 - 23

40s during day,
light frosts.
sifted dirt,
weeded garden, drew
not fully, clipped
leaves, general
clean-up.

Skunned Robin
Witch-hazel
not Arnold's
Promise, 11/23

Hatch of Bluebottle
Flies indoors -
over 3 days, we
got 75 or more.
They sluggishly
fly to windows
in the morning.

1997

15 29.7 S, 30°, cldy,
windy, raw,
flurries

16 29.8 ↓, 30°, clear
bec, ptly cldy

17 30.0 ↑, 20°, clear
40s

18 30.4 ↑, 24°, clear
tree work

19 30.4 ↑, 20°, clear
To Round Pond

21 Return

1998

17   40° at dawn,
drizzle, raw, temp.
drops

NOVEMBER

WEEK 4

WEATHER _____

OUTSIDE

   VEGETABLES _____

   FRUIT _____

   FLOWERS _____

   BULBS _____

   SHRUBS/TREES _____

   LAWNS _____

GREENHOUSE _____

NOTES _____ _____

YEAR 1994

24 Much colder.
18° at dawn

Thanksgiving.
Plum Island
Deer
Ruby-cr. Kinglet
Coot
Merganser
Gr. Yellowlegs
Snow Geese
Canada "
Peregrin
Rafts of Eider

28 1¼" Rain !

29 Mild

YEAR 1995

AWAY

27 Return.

28 Mild,
breezy,
Clumped
leaves

29 2" of snow.
Cold —
Upper 20's

30 18° at dawn

Year	1996	Year	1997	Year	1998

1996

24 Mild. Filled frost-caused depression in lawn, more clean-up.

25 First snow flyin at dawn.

26 Cold

27 Light snow overnight

28 Cold – 15° at dawn, becoming overcast

29 Cold, clear

1997

22 40°, 30.0"s, Rain 1.25" overnight 35° + wet snow by 10 AM. Flurries all day

23 30.25↑, 35°, cldy Lots of juncos!

24 29.9↓, 30°, snow drizzles To Madison for a week

1998

Mild, left or no frost. Scabiosa, Primroses, Snapdragons, Late Mums all still blooming. Nearly all leaves down now.

26 POURING RAIN!

27 Ptly cldy, cool, gusty N.W.

28 Warmer, gusty W-SW

29 40s, mostly sunny

30 42 at dawn

DECEMBER

At Christmas I no more desire a rose

Than wish a snow in May's new-fangled

>   *mirth;*

But like of each thing that in season grows.

WILLIAM SHAKESPEARE
LOVE'S LABOUR'S LOST

Autumn Morning
John Atkinson Grimshaw

DECEMBER

WEEK 1

WEATHER _____

OUTSIDE
    VEGETABLES _____

    FRUIT _____

    FLOWERS _____

    BULBS _____

    SHRUBS/TREES _____

    LAWNS _____

GREENHOUSE _____

NOTES _____

YEAR ...... 1994 ......

Mild

5 1.5" rain
1 whistling swan
with 2 mutes in
bay.
7 More rain;
turning colder,
flurries by
evening

YEAR ...... 1995 ......

6 Rain in
A.M.

7 Cold, blustery

Year 1996	Year 1997	Year 1998

1996

2 Heavy rain
3 } mild, fair
4
5

6 Mix of wet snow
r rain, gusty
NE wind. First
winter storm of
year.

7 Cold drizzle
all day here.
Further, indeed,
6"-18" of snow!
Junco at feeder.
Drenching rain
overnight

Bay: Buffleheads,
Blacks. Salt Pan:
Blacks, Gr. Winged Teal
Hellcat: Yellow-r.
warblers

1997

1 Return from Madison.
Windy, cold day - airport
shut-down for time

2 29.5↑, 25°, strong
NW gusts + wind,
ptly cldy → clear

3 30.0↑, 28°, less wind,
clear

4 29.75↓, 35°, showers
overnight, chng

5 Beautiful. 40-ish

6 29.45↑, 30°, clear,
breezy.

7 29.5↑, 30°, cldy
To R.P. to pack up
house

1998

1 — Warm, sunny,
occ. 60s, dry

2 "

3 "

7 75°!

DECEMBER

WEEK 2

WEATHER _____

OUTSIDE

VEGETABLES _____

FRUIT _____

FLOWERS _____

BULBS _____

SHRUBS/TREES _____

LAWNS _____

GREENHOUSE _____

NOTES _____

YEAR 1994

8   18° at dawn, blustery NW wind.

10 or so – warms up, cloudy, rain, dreary

YEAR 1995

8   18° at dawn again.

9   Snow, changing to rain.

10 Strong bitter winds. 26° at dawn, dropping to 24° at noon.

gorgeous fleece at sunset.

11. Winds 15° at dawn, 25° the high! Flicker, Juncos. Harries on Plumbs.

12 10° at dawn

14 Snow – 6"

YEAR 1996	YEAR 1997	YEAR 1998

1996

8   Sunny, 40°

↓ Rest of week
↓ cool, drizzly.
15

   Many flights
   of Canada
   geese arrive.

1997

8 Round Pond
11 clamp house

11   Return.
     30.4↑, clear

12 30.2↓, 24°, cldy
    → broken clouds

13 29.9↓, 24°, clear

14 29.75↓ 28°, clear
    Strong cold front in
    evening — from 42°
    to 20° in a few hours

1998

8 Cold, raw, rain —
   High 30s

9 Clear, 40s.
   Frost @ dawn

10

   Pretty much
   the same

14

 # DECEMBER

WEEK 3

WEATHER _____

OUTSIDE

   VEGETABLES _____

   FRUIT _____

   FLOWERS _____

   BULBS _____

   SHRUBS/TREES _____

   LAWNS _____

GREENHOUSE _____

NOTES _____

YEAR **1994**

17 Dreary, drizzly.
Heavy rain overnight

18 Drizzle, mid-30s

19 Sunny, mild, windy

22

YEAR **1995**

16 Snow showers.
Tree Sparrow,
Pheasant tracks

17 At least 12" of
snow since
the 15th.
Sunny, upper
20s

19 Bold. Snow
begins at 4 pm

20 20° at dawn.
Snow continued.
About 5-6" fell
by 10 am. Lull
at mid day. Star[ted]
again at 3:00 pm.

Cooper's Hawk
flies overhead —
too big for jay -
sized Sharpshin.

YEAR 1996	YEAR 1997	YEAR 1998

1996

16 Drizzly

17 Downpours - reaches low 50s

18 Fog, then SUN - 50s

19 Cool, drizzly showers

20 Cold front. B4tn, NW wind, great pressure increase.

21 18° at dawn. Crystal clear, 31.4" Hg

1997

15 29.61, 10°, gusty. By features, 30.15, 30°, calm, clear

16 30.1↑, 15°, clear, calm

17 29.95, 25° clear, calm, Hit 50°

18 30.1↑, 25°, clear, calm, 40s

19 30.0 ↓s, 30°, o'cast

20 Boston. Cldy, 40s

21 30.25↑, 16°, clear, NW wind

1998

15 mild

16 mild

17 Raw, rain,

18 First really cold day - gusty NW, 30s

19 - 21 mild

DECEMBER

WEEK 4

WEATHER _____

OUTSIDE

  VEGETABLES _____

  FRUIT _____

  FLOWERS _____

  BULBS _____

  SHRUBS/TREES _____

  LAWNS _____

GREENHOUSE _____

NOTES _____

YEAR **1993-94**

12/22/93 MOVE IN!
Warm, windy, torrential
rains.
Cold snap
before Christmas.

Snow shortly
after — 6" or
so

Mulched Rhododen-
drens after the
first snow,
during a break
in the cold

1994

24 Torrential rain,
gusty winds.
Hurricane-force
winds, 4.75" rain
in Gloucester by 6 PM!

25-28 Mild, fair

29 Strong cold front.
40° at 6 AM,
28 at 11 AM,
gusty NW winds.

30 5° at dawn

YEAR **1995**

21 20° at dawn,
snow showers,
some white-out
all day

23 Mild, some
sun.
2 bald eagles,
1 gt. Bl. Heron
at bridge

24 Mild, some
sun, some flurries
2 Tree Sp. at
feeders

25 Cool, sun in AM.
Eiders, Wh. wing Scoter,
RB Mergansers, common
at north end of the land.
Fed. Sanctuary closed.

26 Raw, cloudy.
27, 28, 29 Pleasant, 30-is
31 Over freezing first time
in a week. Eve clear, cr

XMAS BIRDS - House
Rock Dove, Mourning Dove
Downy, Blue Jay, B-C Chick.
WB Nut, RB Nut, Mockingb
Cardinal, P. Finch, goldfinch
Starling, Junco, Tree Spar
Brown Creeper, mocking bird
Bufflehead, Black, Mall
Eider, Wh. W. Scoter, RB M

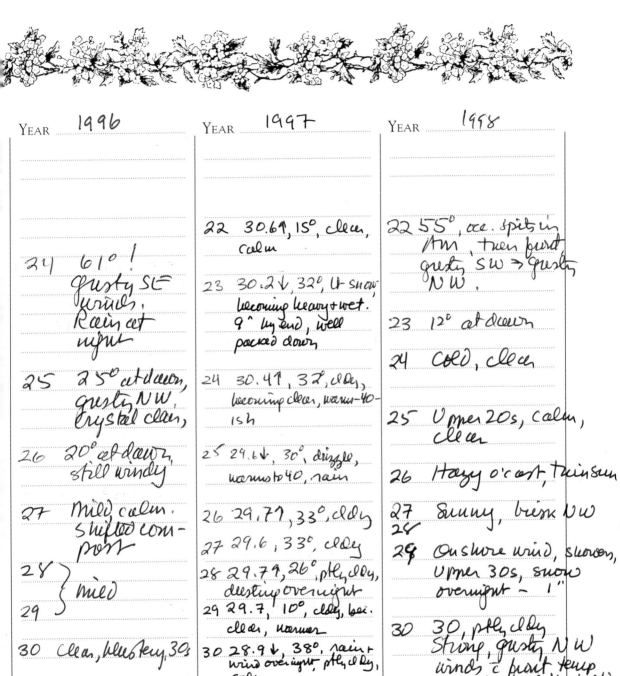

YEAR 1996	YEAR 1997	YEAR 1958
	22 30.6↑, 15°, clear, calm	22 55°, occ. spits in AM, then burst, gusty SW → gusty NW.
24 61°! gusty SE winds, Rain at night	23 30.2↓, 32°, lt snow becoming heavy + wet. 9" by end, well packed down	
		23 12° at dawn
25 25° at dawn, gusty NW, crystal clear,	24 30.4↑, 32°, cldy, becoming clear, warms-40-ish	24 cold, clear
26 20° at dawn, still windy	25 29.6↓, 30°, drizzle, warms to 40, rain	25 Upper 20s, calm, clear
27 Mild, calm. shifted compost	26 29.7↑, 33°, cldy	26 Hazy o'cast, thin sun
	27 29.6, 33°, cldy	27 Sunny, brisk NW 28
28 } mild 29	28 29.7↓, 26°, ptly cldy, dusting overnight	29 Onshore wind, showers, Upper 30s, snow overnight – 1"
	29 29.7, 10°, cldy, bec. clear, warmer	
30 Clear, blustery, 30s	30 28.9↓, 38°, rain + wind overnight, ptly cldy, calm	30 30, ptly cldy strong, gusty NW winds c front, temp drops to 10° by bedtime
31 18° at 5:30AM, 14° at 7:00AM! light snow	31 29.45↑ rapidly, 25°, o'cast	31 –2° at dawn, hazy sun, upper teens, calm

SUMMARY YEAR ONE

	SPRING	SUMMER
WEATHER		
VEGETABLES		
FRUIT		
FLOWERS		
BULBS		
SHRUBS/TREES		
LAWN		
GREENHOUSE		
NEW PLANTS		
EQUIPMENT		
NOTES		

Autumn

Winter

Weather

Vegetables

Fruit

Flowers

Bulbs

Shrubs/Trees

Lawn

Greenhouse

New
Plants

Equipment

Notes

SUMMARY YEAR TWO

	SPRING	SUMMER
WEATHER		
VEGETABLES		
FRUIT		
FLOWERS		
BULBS		
SHRUBS/TREES		
LAWN		
GREENHOUSE		
NEW PLANTS		
EQUIPMENT		
NOTES		

AUTUMN

WINTER

WEATHER

VEGETABLES

FRUIT

FLOWERS

BULBS

SHRUBS/TREES

LAWN

GREENHOUSE

NEW
PLANTS

EQUIPMENT

NOTES

SUMMARY YEAR THREE

	SPRING	SUMMER
WEATHER		
VEGETABLES		
FRUIT		
FLOWERS		
BULBS		
SHRUBS/TREES		
LAWN		
GREENHOUSE		
NEW PLANTS		
EQUIPMENT		
NOTES		

AUTUMN

WINTER

WEATHER

VEGETABLES

FRUIT

FLOWERS

BULBS

SHRUBS/TREES

LAWN

GREENHOUSE

NEW
PLANTS

EQUIPMENT

NOTES

 # SUMMARY YEAR FOUR

	SPRING	SUMMER
WEATHER		
VEGETABLES		
FRUIT		
FLOWERS		
BULBS		
SHRUBS/TREES		
LAWN		
GREENHOUSE		
NEW PLANTS		
EQUIPMENT		
NOTES		

Autumn

Winter

Weather

Vegetables

Fruit

Flowers

Bulbs

Shrubs/Trees

Lawn

Greenhouse

New
Plants

Equipment

Notes

SUMMARY YEAR FIVE

	SPRING	SUMMER
WEATHER		
VEGETABLES		
FRUIT		
FLOWERS		
BULBS		
SHRUBS/TREES		
LAWN		
GREENHOUSE		
NEW PLANTS		
EQUIPMENT		
NOTES		

AUTUMN

WINTER

WEATHER

VEGETABLES

FRUIT

FLOWERS

BULBS

SHRUBS/TREES

LAWN

GREENHOUSE

NEW
PLANTS

EQUIPMENT

NOTES

Garden Suppliers

Name ....
Address ....
....
....
Telephone ....

Name ....
Address ....
....
....
Telephone ....

Name ....
Address ....
....
....
Telephone ....

Name ....
Address ....
....
....
Telephone ....

Name ....
Address ....
....
....
Telephone ....

Name ....
Address ....
....
....
Telephone ....

Name ....
Address ....
....
....
Telephone ....

Name ....
Address ....
....
....
Telephone ....

Name ....
Address ....
....
....
Telephone ....

Name ....
Address ....
....
....
Telephone ....

SEED MERCHANTS

NAME ....

ADDRESS ....

....

....

TELEPHONE ....

NAME ....

ADDRESS ....

....

....

TELEPHONE ....

NAME ....

ADDRESS ....

....

....

TELEPHONE ....

NAME ....

ADDRESS ....

....

....

TELEPHONE ....

NAME ....

ADDRESS ....

....

....

TELEPHONE ....

NAME ....

ADDRESS ....

....

....

TELEPHONE ....

NAME ....

ADDRESS ....

....

....

TELEPHONE ....

NAME ....

ADDRESS ....

....

....

TELEPHONE ....

NAME ....

ADDRESS ....

....

....

TELEPHONE ....

NAME ....

ADDRESS ....

....

....

TELEPHONE ....

HERB SUPPLIERS

NAME

ADDRESS

TELEPHONE

NAME

ADDRESS

TELEPHONE

NAME

ADDRESS

TELEPHONE

NAME

ADDRESS

TELEPHONE

NAME

ADDRESS

TELEPHONE

NAME

ADDRESS

TELEPHONE

NAME

ADDRESS

TELEPHONE

NAME

ADDRESS

TELEPHONE

NAME

ADDRESS

TELEPHONE

NAME

ADDRESS

TELEPHONE

ROSE SUPPLIERS

NAME

ADDRESS

TELEPHONE

NAME

ADDRESS

TELEPHONE

NAME

ADDRESS

TELEPHONE

NAME

ADDRESS

TELEPHONE

NAME

ADDRESS

TELEPHONE

NAME

ADDRESS

TELEPHONE

NAME

ADDRESS

TELEPHONE

NAME

ADDRESS

TELEPHONE

NAME

ADDRESS

TELEPHONE

NAME

ADDRESS

TELEPHONE

ORNAMENTAL TREE & SHRUB SUPPLIERS

NAME

ADDRESS

TELEPHONE

NAME

ADDRESS

TELEPHONE

NAME

ADDRESS

TELEPHONE

NAME

ADDRESS

TELEPHONE

NAME

ADDRESS

TELEPHONE

NAME

ADDRESS

TELEPHONE

NAME

ADDRESS

TELEPHONE

NAME

ADDRESS

TELEPHONE

NAME

ADDRESS

TELEPHONE

NAME

ADDRESS

TELEPHONE

BULB SUPPLIERS

NAME ....

ADDRESS ....

....

....

TELEPHONE ....

NAME ....

ADDRESS ....

....

....

TELEPHONE ....

NAME ....

ADDRESS ....

....

....

TELEPHONE ....

NAME ....

ADDRESS ....

....

....

TELEPHONE ....

NAME ....

ADDRESS ....

....

....

TELEPHONE ....

NAME ....

ADDRESS ....

....

....

TELEPHONE ....

NAME ....

ADDRESS ....

....

....

TELEPHONE ....

NAME ....

ADDRESS ....

....

....

TELEPHONE ....

NAME ....

ADDRESS ....

....

....

TELEPHONE ....

NAME ....

ADDRESS ....

....

....

TELEPHONE ....

OTHER SPECIALIST SUPPLIERS

NAME ....

ADDRESS ....

....

....

TELEPHONE ....

NAME ....

ADDRESS ....

....

....

TELEPHONE ....

NAME ....

ADDRESS ....

....

....

TELEPHONE ....

NAME ....

ADDRESS ....

....

....

TELEPHONE ....

NAME ....

ADDRESS ....

....

....

TELEPHONE ....

NAME ....

ADDRESS ....

....

....

TELEPHONE ....

NAME ....

ADDRESS ....

....

....

TELEPHONE ....

NAME ....

ADDRESS ....

....

....

TELEPHONE ....

NAME ....

ADDRESS ....

....

....

TELEPHONE ....

NAME ....

ADDRESS ....

....

....

TELEPHONE ....

OTHER SPECIALIST SUPPLIERS

NAME

ADDRESS

TELEPHONE

NAME

ADDRESS

TELEPHONE

NAME

ADDRESS

TELEPHONE

NAME

ADDRESS

TELEPHONE

NAME

ADDRESS

TELEPHONE

NAME

ADDRESS

TELEPHONE

NAME

ADDRESS

TELEPHONE

NAME

ADDRESS

TELEPHONE

NAME

ADDRESS

TELEPHONE

NAME

ADDRESS

TELEPHONE

Approximate Measures
For Gardeners

Length/Width
A hand (closed) = 4 inches
A hand (spread) = 7-8 inches
A foot = 10-12 inches
Finger-tip to elbow = 18 inches
Finger-tip to opposite shoulder = 3 feet 3 inches (1 metre)
A pace (stride) = 3 feet

Area
Acre = 70 paces x 70 paces
Hectare = 2½ acres

Liquid Volume
1 teaspoonful = 4 ml
1 dessertspoonful = 8 ml
1 tablespoonful = 16 ml (½ fluid ounce)
2 tablespoonfuls = 32 ml (1 fluid ounce)
Household bucket = 2 gallons (9 litres)

Manure/Compost
1 barrow load = 10 lbs (enough for 10 sq yds/90 sq ft)
– i.e. 30 ft x 3 ft or 15 ft x 6 ft

Trees
Age – Circumference of tree (inches) = age of tree (years)
Height = distance of observer from tree when angle from observer's
eye to tree top is approx 45°